LESBIAN LETTERS

LESBIAN LETTERS

By Christine Heron Stockton

HERON
PRESS

SAN FRANCISCO

Published by:
Heron Press
P.O. Box 31539
San Francisco, Ca. 94131

First Edition
Printed in the U.S.A.

Designed by Dorothy Remington
Photos by Holly Stewart
Typesetting by QuadraType
Printing by McNaughton & Gunn

ISBN 0-935999-01-9
Library of Congress Catalog Card Number: 85-82028

TABLE OF CONTENTS

PREFACE

CHAPTER I—COMING OUT TO SELF

CHAPTER II—COMING OUT TO FAMILY

CHAPTER V—THE COMMUNITY

ACKNOWLEDGMENTS

PREFACE

I recall as a teenager that one of the worst names to be called in school was "queer." No one really knew what it meant, yet it was used a lot and was certainly a nasty thing to be. The only other reference to homosexuality I remember during my childhood was my mother's hilarious imitation of her lisping hairdresser, who was "light on his feet." We children laughed a lot at that.

In my early twenties, I thought that homosexuals were limp-wristed men or very mannish women who did something bad and mysterious with members of their own sex. But to my astonishment a few years later, I found myself strongly attracted to certain women. These feelings I had camouflaged from myself and others for a long time. After all, *I* was nothing like the stereotype of a lesbian. Yet these feelings kept surfacing and so I bravely began to meet women who were lesbians. I was surprised to discover that they were as diverse and as normal as straight women. I soon gravitated to my natural sexual orientation and called myself a lesbian. Sexually and intimately I felt at home for the first time in my life. But what had happened to the stereotype? It had vanished for me, yet I noticed it was still very real for society. I now saw this stereotype of lesbians as an illusion causing fear, degradation, and much pain on both "sides." I wrote this book to cut through that illusion and to help heal the separation between heterosexual and homosexual "worlds."

Written in the form of fictional letters and journal entries, this book is about the lives of lesbians: the difficulty in recognizing one's lesbianism, the trauma of coming out to one's family, the questions around lesbians parenting, lesbians in their love relationships, and the struggle of the lesbian community for acceptance in society. These areas are explored in five chapters by lesbians, their families, and their friends writing of their experiences.

Some of the letters are exchanges between people; some are singular; and those of one woman, Jennifer, appear throughout the book. The letters were not written sequentially and can be read in any order one wishes. There is no plot, there are no long stories in this book. Rather, it establishes a context for the humanness, the real life concerns, and the courage of ordinary women dealing with a sexuality different from society's "norm."

Chapter One explores the stirrings caused by being attracted to someone of the same sex. The teenage crush is not always just a phase and can lead to confusion and painful rejection when the desire is first acted on. Women who do act on their attraction to other women have different experiences: some become bisexual, some vacillate out of fear, and some accept their homosexuality and the name lesbian.

In Chapter Two women write about what is usually the most terrifying aspect of coming out for them: telling their parents. It is a personal decision for each woman when and if to come out to her parents and one that risks much in their relationship. The reactions of parents range from acceptance, to avoidance, to disownment.

Chapter Three deals with the issues facing many lesbians who have or want to have children. A mother agonizes over whether or not to come out to her teenage children. A four-part family correspondence starts with the oldest daughter writing to her parents that she is pregnant by donor insemination. Her parents respond with great concern, her younger sister with a strong religious condemnation of a fatherless family.

Chapter Four contains a variety of writings about lesbians

in their intimate relationships. These women speak in poetry and love letters, of their hurt and loneliness, of their passion and romantic involvements—expressions of the human desire to partner.

In Chapter Five, lesbians write about the controversial issues and the environment of their community. The letters cover social gatherings, the constant struggle against legal and religious discrimination, how they deal with death, their values and spirituality.

The women is this book voice the concerns of all homosexuals, which are indeed the same as those of all human beings: love, family, community, health, work, relationship to God and to oneself. It is my intention that the derision, the fear, the stereotypes of homosexuals we all acquire in childhood will dissolve as we come together in acknowledgment of our humanity.

Christine Heron Stockton

October 1985

Chapter I
COMING OUT TO SELF

FIRST CRUSH

Nov. 25, 1963

Dear Vicky,

Today Hillary smiled at me three times—and actually asked how I was doing!!! I made an excuse to go to the back of Big Study Hall to see my sister Susan when she was studying. As I talked to Susan my heart was going crazy with Hillary right behind me. Finally I got up the courage to turn in her direction. She looked up and gave me that fantastic smile—so warm I could feel it all over. I thought I was going to faint when she said, "How are you Nina?" I somehow said "fine," though my heart was pounding so fast I didn't think I could speak. Her eyes are so big and blue, like the sky on a clear day. I like the way her beautiful blond hair is pulled up behind her head with a braid over her forehead. It makes her look sort of foreign, Swedish.

Out of nowhere I got the brilliant idea to ask her who was going to win the Gym Meet this year (she's the Green Team Captain) and she said, "The Greens of course!" I said, "Maybe not. I'm a White and we have a pretty good team." "No chance," she said, and then "Got to run to class, see ya!" and a quick smile as she went down the aisle. Her legs are so muscular and the curve of her hip under the white blouse as she walked down the aisle—too much! And as she left study hall I remembered I was supposed to be seeing Susan. I turned and found her looking at me strangely—got to be more cool around big sister. But to have actually talked to HER! I think about her all the time—she's a dream! I wish I were a Green so I could be closer to her during the Gym Meet. Hillary actually talked to me today!!! Those blue eyes going right into me. I wonder what excuse I can dream up to talk to her again soon. I get crazy just being near her and today we

1

talked natural, a seventh-grader to a senior, but not just *any* senior. I think I'm in love!!!

Mrs. Sharp is driving me nuts with her damn Latin conjugations! I'll make it through Christmas somehow, but I can't wait to see you then when we visit the grandparents! Have you heard the latest Peter, Paul and Mary album? I'll bring it with me. Write soon!

Love Nina

P.S. When you saw Hillary that once on your last visit, didn't you think she was the most beautiful girl you'd ever seen?

DUAL CRUSH

Jan. 26, 1968

Dear Diary,

The school dance last night was okay, but what a hassle afterward! Frank just couldn't keep his hands from trying to get in my pants no matter how many times I said no. Why don't guys understand when I say no I mean it? I try not to hurt their feelings or encourage them, but they always try to push on. It ticks me off and it ruined the evening for him and me.

There we were, parked on the farm road on a freezing night, my chest with goosebumps on top of goosebumps, and he's trying to get my pants off. Finally, I just had to shove him away. He got angry and drove me home fast, roaring out the driveway as he left. God knows what Mom and Dad thought. They were kind and didn't even ask me how my evening was. Godamnit, I like him, but not enough to go to third base. I wonder if he'll want to go out with me again—I don't really care, but I have fun seeing movies with him and doubling with friends. We'll see . . . .

I forgot to write about last Friday. During gym class, Miss Lawton was out on the playing field, quite a distance from me. For the hell of it, I made a snowball and heaved it as hard as I could in her direction. And (shock) it hit her square on the top of her head! I ran, but she caught up with me at the gym door and we wrestled, laughing hysterically. She was angry, yet she looked so ridiculous with snow dripping down her head that she had to laugh. She chewed me out royally before admitting I was a good shot. I was so embarrassed and yet secretly pleased by her attention.

I offered to help dry her hair. She said no, but let me hang around while she cleaned up. I watched her undo her bun and was stunned as a wave of luxurious black hair fell to her waist. I never knew it was so long and I watched her comb out the damp snarls as we talked. She is so beautiful and feminine. Her dark almond eyes and dark skin next to that cascade of hair was a sight! When she turned she smiled at me, her perfect white teeth shining out of the dark. I was suddenly very warm and slightly uncomfortable, even though there was no place on earth I'd rather have been at that moment.

She is my ideal woman—smart, gorgeous, athletic (her tall, slim body is dynamite), and really nice. I feel like a klutz next to her. And she's mysterious, too. She keeps telling us all she's a Blackfoot Indian, and that's where she gets her dark complexion and hair from, but with a name like Miss Lawton, that doesn't fit. She likes to tease us all. Anyway, after her hair was dry, she snapped me with the towel and said I'd better watch out for snowballs in the future! We laughed and I watched her go down the hall. My heartbeat finally slowed and I turned to the locker room for a shower. Heavenly encounter with Miss Carolyn Lawton!

March 20, 1973

Dear Roz,

Hi there! I've been back here in Albany now for a week and already my tan is fading like crazy! It's freezing here and a snowstorm is forecasted for tonight. Shit! It's hard to think we were in the Bahamas just a week ago. I miss the miles of pink beach, the turquoise sea, and the reggae band at Little Joe's. I guess we all had to come back to reality sooner or later.

So how's school? You must be busy with end-of-the-year papers and graduation coming up. Are you doing the works with your parents coming in from N.Y.C. and all? And what are you up to this summer? I'm trying to get a job training as a heart-lung technician at a hospital here, but so far, no luck. So I'm just hanging out here at home and spending a lot of time with my boyfriend Stan. It still seems strange not to be in school after so long.

About what happened—please don't be freaked out by it. I still don't understand myself what was going on, but I never meant to scare you. As I said that night, I just had, and had for some days, an overwhelming desire to kiss you. It came out of the blue for me and grew to such a point I just had to tell you about it. I don't blame you for getting upset. I just wanted to kiss you, and the feeling was so strong I just had to tell you about it or burst. It's not that I'm a lesbian or anything—I have a boyfriend and we're doing fine. I just really liked you, our talks, and the fun I had with you down there. Maybe it was too much sun or rum at the club, but I began to get this urge to kiss you, and I must admit, I thought I would go batty if I didn't at least tell you about it. I understand your reaction and your fear. I would have done the same. But when you backed off I did wonder whether the fear in your eyes was that you might have enjoyed it if you had allowed yourself. When you got really distant and pulled away those last few days, not wanting to talk about it, that hurt a little—actually more than a little because I was so confused.

I would like to keep in touch with you and maybe even visit you in N.Y.C. this summer, if I don't have a job. I promise I won't get weird on you. I would just like to further our friendship. We did have a lot of fun until that night. Again, I don't understand what happened and would like to forget it happened. Okay? Let me know how the end of school is for you and where you'll be this summer. Maybe we can get together.

Every time I hear "I Can See Clearly Now," I recall your belting it out with the band at Joe's and the whole gang carousing around on those warm nights. It went too fast and now there's snow to deal with. So much for spring vacation!

Take care,

CHRIS

March 30, 1973

Dear Chris,

    I have found myself sitting and thinking about vacation and your letter for a long time. I am no author, so excuse the way this letter is written. It is something I have to do because I am not at all at ease and I don't want to leave things hanging. I'm at a loss about where to start. I guess I might as well begin by saying that although I have been as I am for a couple of years, and knowing that even I didn't like it, this vacation was the first time anyone had actually confronted me and asked what I was doing. By "being as I am," I mean aloof from all problems and keeping myself closed up in a shell. I got that shell for protection because I had been shot down so many times. I felt that it was the only way I could keep myself together, and I plainly have not let go of it because I seemed so happy, yet wasn't. I was afraid of what might happen if I opened up. I now see I must do so, but I want to do it slowly so I won't wind up right back where I started. And it is people like you who make me immediately put my defenses back up. It is one of the only ways I know to cope.

    Now, about my feelings. You really shocked the hell out of me. As honestly as possible, I have never even dreamed or had a flicker of thought of being anything but heterosexual. I've never been attracted sexually to a female. This is not putting my defenses up, either. The fear you saw in my eyes was not the fear that I might like kissing you. I knew clearly that I didn't even want to try it. It really turned me off.

    ENOUGH!

    Let's get off that track! How's life? Wheaton is not exactly hopping. I went to Dartmouth to see my boyfriend last weekend.

It was great seeing him because he was in Mexico winter term. Next weekend is Fathers' Weekend and in June, graduation at last. My brother is also coming for that, which will be fun. Signing off and out.

Later,

Feb. 28, 1976

Dear Martin,

Remember the conversation/battle we had all across Asia and in particular, the night when we stayed up until 3 a.m. in Kabul wreathed in hash smoke? Well, I hate to admit it, but with your forceful badgering, my heterosexual-finding-one-man-marriage-monogamy-the-rest-of-my-life-normalcy picture has melted down. You were right, there are more choices in life, and I've begun investigating another avenue. One month ago I had my first affair with a woman! I bet even you, you licentious fag, are a bit shocked that your straight WASP girlfriend is trying the other side of the fence. But don't take too much credit, darling heart, the underground desire had always been there, and you and our wonderful trip to the ends of the earth helped bring the desire aboveground.

Yes, I slept with a woman, not just once but as much as I could! And Martin, it was heaven, a whole other ball game. I was so excited I could barely stand it. At last I was able to fully let loose sexually and it was grand! She is an old college friend of mine. Her name is Bonnie. My friend Doris, another college chum, and I went to visit her up in San Francisco. The moment I laid eyes on her, I somehow knew she was a lesbian (don't ask me how I knew, for I'd never consciously laid eyes on "one" before) and she knew I knew. She came out to us eventually and Doris was pretty upset and talked a lot. I kept quiet and when Doris was in the bathroom the second night, I got up my nerve and kissed Bonnie thoroughly. I thought we both were going to fall over from surprise. After that I was a woman possessed, but we couldn't do anything with Doris there so . . . the next weekend I drove up to

Carmel Valley and we had a lost weekend in bed at her parents' house while they were away. And the next weekend and the next I flew up north to be with her. But by the third weekend, we realized something was missing. Even though we had a great time in bed, we really weren't what the other was looking for in a relationship, so we parted amicably.

For me, though, the doors are now open. It's funny because I haven't shut off men, I am just less attached to them. I truly feel as if I can make a choice, and the freedom is terrific! I also feel that everyone has this choice. We are all bisexual, only most of us refuse to accept it because of our upbringing and the fear of being considered abnormal. We don't realize that it is the most natural state of all. So where I am now, I can realize my wholeness and my attraction for women and men. I want a deep relationship, one in which I really share myself and my life with another person and I don't care if it's a man or a woman. I'm tired at age 26 of short-term affairs. Pretty neat, eh?

And you? The other half of our conversation/battle was my badgering you about the worthwhileness of tricking with a different man every night. Is that what you really want? From my point of view, it seems to make sex, which is so wonderful, so cheap. Don't you ever want an ongoing relationship where sex and love can grow and get better and better? Now that I've turned the corner, I encourage you to do the same. We aren't getting any younger! (I know, nag, nag, nag—that's my job.)

Are you ever going to move out here? I miss you like crazy. There is no one like you in the whole world and certainly no one who understands me as well, or me you for that matter. Who in White Plains could see with you the gorgeous dung-smoke sunsets of Khajraho and the magical sunrise on the high desert of Afghanistan, or recapture the glory of 9 o'clock Western Civ. class senior year? No one, dear heart. Come West—you'll find a job, there is plenty of action here, and we'll have great fun!

Write back soon. I'm curious to learn your reaction to the sexual monster you've unleashed! Seriously, I am very happy and feel fully alive and free for the first time in my life. Thank you so very much for opening up those possibilities for me. I treasure your love, dear friend. Now get your ass out here!

Love Jennifer

COMING OUT TO SELF

WHAT AM I?

May 3, 1981

Dear Gladys,

Hope you and Bob and the kids are well. I still miss you horribly even though it's been two years since you moved. Boca Raton seems like another world away when I need to talk to someone, and the phone drives me crazy, knowing the dollars click off as I talk, so pen and paper it is.

What I want to talk about is hard, because I'm so confused about it. Remember when I left Roy last fall and had a brief encounter with that woman? You said it was just a stage coming after such a rotten marriage and that I'd start seeing men again once I was away from him for a while. Well, Gladys, I haven't been with a man even for a date since (just once, and it was a flop). In fact, I've been sneaking out to women's bars. I'm scared to tell you this because I'm afraid you'll think I'm a lesbian. That word drives me nuts. It is so stereotyped and far from me, far from my home environment, and yet I find myself enjoying the company of gay women. And Gladys, this really scares me—I'm sexually attracted to some of them. I haven't slept with any of them since Robin, for fear of the kids or someone finding out, but also, to be truthful, I'm terrified I'll like it too much. I find myself looking at women far more than at men, and in fact, I am repulsed when a man comes on to me now. Remember how turned on to guys I was in high school? I don't understand this shift and I don't think it's just my hatred of Roy. But Gladys, a lesbian lifestyle is so different from mine with three kids and a house in suburbia. I couldn't possibly abandon all I have or tell anyone but you. I trust you because you're my best friend and have known me since Garfield Grammar. Most of my other friends here I've lost interest in since the breakup. I somehow see them as shallow now. I'm so confused because I feel safe, stronger, and desired as a person, not just as a "dame," by these new women friends, but I'm an upstanding straight housewife from Middle America Detroit, for Christ's sake. I'm living a double life and feel terribly pulled in both directions. Janice asked me the other day if I had a secret boyfriend because she's seen me coming in late and I blushed and stammered some idiot excuse and went inside quickly. And my new friends ask me if I'm "bi" or what, and I don't know how to respond.

I'm particularly pressed now because there's this terrific woman named Angela. When I'm around her I kind of get weak in the knees and act like a teenager. She's been asking me to dance and we talk a lot, especially about kids. She has one daughter and I get the definite impression (but much more subtle than from a guy) that she'd like to come home with me. She's intelligent, a very kind person, and a coach at the college so she's in good shape. Each time it gets harder and harder to say no, but I'm just not ready to jump off the cliff (that's what it feels like). If I am a homosexual (and I'm not saying I am yet), I still could never tell the kids, Mom and Dad, or the people at work (I have a part-time job now at that little boutique at Spruce and Clay, The Dress Up), or anyone in my "normal" life. I know if I continue to go to the bar and see Angela I will sleep with her—I want to desperately—I really like (love?) her. I need that closeness, but the labels of dyke/lesbian/queer all make me extremely uncomfortable. After all I may want to be with a man again. I can't see adopting permanently a secretive life and if the word got out . . . I would be crushed by the gossip, probably fired, and Roy, the bastard, would go for the kids. But it's what keeps me sane and whole now, being with these women, being with Angela, and I can't ignore that. I can't understand why my feelings are "wrong" according to society. I don't fit anymore, anywhere.

HELP! Please write and give me some of your sensible advice, for I have no one to turn to here and the strain is becoming unbearable. I have dear Angela to talk to and she's very understanding, but I also need someone from my "straight" life to give me some advice.

Tell Beth that Sandy misses her too, but not as much as I miss you, especially now when my reality is very shaky.

Your confused friend,

Tommy

COMING OUT TO SELF

BI-TO-BYE STRAIGHT

Nov. 10, 1979

Dear Ellen,

Howdy! How's life in the mighty nation of Texas? I'm great and since you, old friend, have known my dating history from the top, I thought I'd run my latest revelation by you. For the last three years, as you know, I have considered myself bisexual, dating both men and women without leaning toward a preference. That's been the honest truth. And believe me, it was hard. Straight people thought I was gay and afraid to cop to it, and lesbians thought I was having a lark and would go back to men. The pressure was intense at times, but I managed to stay sane and felt free actually having no set preference.

I saw James almost exclusively for most of last year and in fact was considering moving in with him. I love him a great deal, but I had to admit I wasn't in love with him and would still go to women's bars occasionally to hang out and dance. He wasn't thrilled with that, but accepted it. Then, two months ago, I met this woman at a bar, and my heart and body went wild. Her name is Sophia, and we had an intense evening of dancing (the slow dances were exquisite torture), but she had to go home to her "roommate." She said their relationship was about over, but her lover was still trying to hang on and Sophia was in the process of trying to get out gracefully. I was frustrated but we managed to meet about once a week and she was all I could think about in between. Two Saturdays ago, we finally made love. Ellen, I'm *in* love—I've never felt this excited emotionally as well as physically. She's beautiful, intelligent, and exciting—everything I've been looking for. Much as I love James, I don't have the electric feeling and the jolt in my heart as I have with Sophia. She pretty much

17

feels the same way, and I'm floating on air.

Now during the past two months, I've been honest with James and we've slowly stopped being lovers. He's been very understanding, but I know it's rough on him. He really wants a marriage. I will always love him, but it really wasn't there for me, a long-term commitment.

But, for the first time, I feel Sophia is "it," and I'm excited and scared at the same time. If she's "it," the scary part then is that I have to be content being a lesbian. I was surprised at my reluctance to call myself one at first; it's such a highly charged word and category. Ideally there would be no labels, but let's face it, the world sees it pretty black and white. So I've had to look at it as the world does, given that I want Sophia for my partner. And honestly, I've looked at all the possible consequences and my feelings and yes, I am willing and indeed choose to be a lesbian. My physical attraction to men has dissolved into uninterest and I feel clearly homosexual. Being bisexual was true for me, and maybe it was a stepping stone to my deeper feelings for women, or I just had to make a choice and it was women. I don't know, but I do know I love Sophia and want to spend the rest of my life with her and have let go of the underlying fear of what the world will think. Since I've let go, I've felt very calm and sure of myself and the word lesbian doesn't now make me squirm (as a matter of fact I'm kind of enjoying it for I do love women and their energy).

Now I can tell you're shaking your head, Ellen, but just know it's the truth for me and don't worry about the label. It doesn't mean I hate men or can't relate to you "breeders" (slang for straight people) as lovingly as I always have. I'll let you know how things progress in my "new world/lifestyle/consciousness," but be assured I'm very much in love and happy (much more so than with Hank, that creepy Romeo back in Houston). In fact, Sophia and I last night talked about moving in together soon. I'm ecstatic! I just have to be patient and wait until she pries herself away from her ex-lover. It's a tricky thing, for they did spend three years together and Sophia doesn't want to hurt her.

Write me soon with your news. Is my godchild teething yet? My love to your parents, and Dick, but most of it goes to you!

Much Love,

Marley

Chapter II
COMING OUT TO FAMILY
TIME TO TELL

May 16, 1983

Dear Mom and Dad,

Hope all is well with you! I'm enjoying the wonderful weather of a sunny San Francisco spring but I do miss the dogwood, the new green of Ohio, and the lambs in the lower pasture. My life is fast and furious right now, lots of projects and social activities, and it's hard to find time even to clean my little apartment! It is important, however, for me to take this time to write to you, especially this letter.

What I want to tell you is most difficult and it's necessary. I am more than a little nervous. That doesn't mean it has to be difficult, so I'll just plunge in and be as honest as I can, heart pounding and all. I am a lesbian. Now, not being there to see or hear your reaction, I'll just talk about what that means to me and how I hope you will feel, given this information.

First of all, I consider myself a human being first, a woman second, and my sexuality is maybe fourth or fifth on the priority list of who I am. And my sexuality, as you now know, is different from the norm—and that doesn't mean it is more important than who my bigger self is.

I am attracted to women and have been so from the start (somehow I don't imagine that's a huge surprise to you). And some years ago, after years of stale relationships with men, I discovered this new realm with women that contained all the elements that had been missing in my intimate relationships. With all choices before me, I soon recognized that I was much more drawn to women, emotionally and physically. My sexuality is a natural part of me and I am glad to have realized it, accepted it, and now love it, for it makes my life whole.

21

If you are now trying to psychoanalyze where you "went wrong" with me, i.e., something you said or did that made me this way, forget it please. Believe me, I had those fears that something strange in my childhood contributed to my homosexuality. I sat myself down and honestly looked at my childhood, at my relationship and interactions with you, and how I was with Julie, Helen, and Ann, and how I was with the whole family. And you know, after half an hour of ruthless scrutiny, I discovered nothing caused me to be a homosexual. I just turned out this way. I see my childhood as normal and wonderful and containing the normal childhood traumas, but so what? I discovered that those psychological fears were fed to us by generations of Freudian analysts, whose self-appointed task was to "cure" us. In the past ten years these same analysts have suddenly "discovered" that homosexuality is not usually a result of trauma or a sickness, but a perfectly valid way of being. The "sickness" myth, however, still persists in society in many forms and I encourage you not to buy into it. Another question that I had to answer for myself before really "coming out" was: "Am I prepared to fall in love and live the rest of my life with a woman and be identified as a lesbian?" Lesbian is such a loaded word. I saw that there might be uncomfortable times with people who got stuck with that label and the fear that society has put on it. Yet I could not deny my natural way of being, and so have chosen to deal with whatever comes and that includes your reaction to my coming out to you.

I have put off telling you for some time because I have feared your disapproval. With all the controversy that homosexuality seems to generate, I know you could never be blasé about it. But I believe I can risk telling you now because I am more confident of who I am as a human being and a lesbian. I want to share my life with you and trust you will accept it, even if you don't understand right away. I give you the problem of what to do if your friends and the whole village "know" about me. I suggest that you first become confident and comfortable about my homosexuality before you discuss it with others. Then what they think is what they think and your reaction can come from understanding rather than from the fear of defending, justifying, or seeing it as a problem. Like every child, I want you to be proud of me and hope that that includes my living happily with a different sexual preference.

Another common myth, and one that prevented me from realizing I was homosexual for so long, is that all lesbians are overweight, unattractive women who try to act like men and yet hate them. Perhaps some women fit that description, but in general, lesbians are as mixed a bag as heterosexuals. All of my lesbian friends are attractive, successful, intelligent women—the same type of women friends I'd have if I were straight. My last lover was a lovely woman who was a debutante in Atlanta. So much for stereotypes!

If you're worried about my emotional health in terms of relationships or society, don't be. First of all, I don't dislike men. I just don't want them as intimate partners. I have many gay and straight male friends as well as gay and straight female friends. I don't discriminate, at least not in terms of their sexuality! All of my friends, old and new, know I'm gay now, as well as Julie, Helen, and Ann, and no one has ever gotten strange about it. I'm still the same person. I have had a couple of relationships with women over the years, but none has developed into a lasting bond. Having had relationships with men for many years and comparing them to my romantic life with lesbians now, I see nothing significantly different between homosexual and hetero-sexual relationships. The same joys, traumas, and emotional interweavings are there no matter whom you're with. I am looking for someone to share my life with, a life partner, a marriage, whatever you want to call it. You both have provided me with a wonderful model of a union that works (though I know it's hard sometimes), and I know I can find that with a woman. My past relationships have taught me what works and what doesn't work in terms of the kind of person I'm compatible with. It will come.

My life is really rather normal and the only thing I see that makes gay relationships a little more difficult than heterosexual ones is society's preoccupation with our difference and reluctance to acknowledge our life unions. I believe that not having the usual structure of marriage allows us great flexibility in how we set up our relationships, i.e., no strict roles or ways of being with each other. And without society's wholehearted sanction, legally or culturally, it is harder when the going gets tough (and it always does) to keep the commitment strong. That is slowly changing, thank God, through more knowledge and communication. Speaking of God, I've gone back to being an active member of the Church since I've discovered it really doesn't exclude homosexuals (at least not in this city). After all, Jesus was here to preach unconditional love. That has been a nice revelation and comfort to me.

So, Mom and Dad, I really sympathize with what this knowledge may entail for you. Just know that it doesn't change one iota of our love for each other, that again nothing about it is your or my fault, and that I am really, truly happy with myself and all my relationships. The one big missing piece had been not telling you and I'm tired of the avoidance and lies. I want you to share in my life and happiness totally, and so it's important you know about my sexuality. Please write or call and feel free to ask or say anything you want about my being a lesbian. It's important that we educate each other and talk about it. You've done a perfect job being my parents, I'm turning out great, and I thank you for all you have given me.

I love you very very much,
Jennifer

P.S. Mom, I know you're mad that homosexuals have taken over your favorite word, "gay." Sorry, but now you can always use it on me!

May 26, 1983

Dearest Jennifer,

We are very moved by your letter, which, as you said, must have been difficult to write. We applaud your courage in writing to us honestly about your sexual preference, which we now know is different from most. Your father and I are not quite sure exactly how to respond to your being a lesbian. We have had many emotions since reading your letter, but always know we love you whatever your choices are in life.

It seems our lot in life as parents is to be concerned about you children, to hope that the rough spots aren't too rough and that you all are happy in your different lives, even now that you are young adults. And frankly we are a little worried about your being homosexual, for homosexuality is controversial and not generally accepted in our society. You seem to have created a well-balanced life in San Francisco, which, as everyone knows, has a large gay population. We are glad you are happy there, and we do miss you, being so far away. Here in Wrights Mills homosexuality just doesn't enter the village scene, and we know very few open homosexuals in Cleveland, period. So mostly what we know about "gays" (you're right, I'm mad they took that delightful word from its proper use!) comes from the press, TV, and yes, the old stereotypes you say are invalid. Now knowing you are a lesbian brings it closer to home and all the gay rights issues have more importance and meaning for us. The AIDS epidemic scares us half to death and we wonder if you risk exposure living in San Francisco and knowing gay men. As far as we know AIDS affects mostly men, but please be careful. It is a gruesome disease and we hope you and your friends are safe.

You're right that it wasn't totally out of the blue for us to learn that you are a lesbian, especially since you settled in San Francisco. Your father and I wondered on occasion, "What if . . . ?" You said in your letter that nothing we or you did in your childhood "made" you homosexual. That is a relief to us since everyone seems to blame parents for everything. However, it's still a challenge not to scrutinize our behavior and wonder if we had done certain things differently, you would have turned out heterosexual (not that homosexual is bad, mind you). You always were a private and different child, hard to understand and cope with, yet very, very special in our hearts. We take your word that you just are that way. We did the best we could with all of you.

We learned a few years ago, and wondered if you knew, that Uncle Charles was homosexual. It is sad to think how hard a conventional marriage must have been on both him and Aunt Louise. He adored the girls, but Aunt Louise was bitter about it, as well she might have been, even after he died. Now that there is more openness about homosexuality, we hope that this kind of mismatch doesn't happen as often.

We are glad you discovered it fairly early and didn't get married to a man out of convention, have children, and then find out it was not for you. And, we are a little sad, for it seems you don't want children and the kind of family life we have had. Our marriage has been wonderful with its ups and downs and we are pleased you hold us as a model for what you want in a "marriage." We truly hope you find the person who will give you the happiness we have had. Know that although it may be awkward at first, we welcome anyone you might want to bring home. We will be coming out to California this fall and want to meet your friends.

It may take some time for us to adjust fully to your being a lesbian, but you expressed yourself so honestly and openly that our concern is minor, especially compared to the love and now respect we have for you. We are indeed proud of you and thank you for taking the risk in sharing your "whole self." Write soon and take good care of yourself.

We love you very very much too!

Mom

+ DAD

P.S. Don't forget Julie's birthday is next week!

COMING OUT TO FAMILY

MIRACLE AT 37

April 23,1985

Dear Ruth,

My father and stepmother just left after a three-day visit and I can't believe the transformation that happened to us. It started the first day when they were looking at my photo board, full of women of course, from Greta Garbo to all my friends and lovers. They asked who the cute blond was with me, and before I had time to think, I was telling them about Jane, my first lover— the whole story start to finish—how hard it was to come out, how lonely and fearful I was because I didn't feel I could tell anyone, and how much it hurt when we broke up at the end of school. And then I went through the whole board talking about these women in my past, which had only been a shadow with Dad and Gloria.

They had known, of course, all these years and I had known they'd known, but I was so afraid of their overt disapproval and they, so afraid of broaching the taboo subject, that for 37 years we've played this ridiculous avoidance game. I didn't have a love life to speak of. I was the oddball, the rebel, the ungrateful daughter, but never the queer. But Ruth, after my long exposé of my love life, they just smiled and hugged me. We were all so moved we almost cried. In retrospect, I can't believe that I, a successful accountant, writer, and businesswoman, was so scared of Dad and Gloria. It's amazing the fantasies and fears we hold onto from the past. It was so easy and it feels so good to be out with it, open and all of me with them. I even like my classic Jewish father more. I accept him now as he is. The real proof of his acceptance came when we were out to brunch at the Pier with my friend, Lois the Doctor. When she went to the bathroom he said, "Why don't you marry her, she's a nice girl and a doctor?!" We all cracked up and I felt so marvelous as I moaned "Daaad"!

I've never asked you about how you are with your parents. I've gathered you weren't overtly out with them, but after last weekend, I highly recommend allowing them into your life. We usually don't give parents credit for understanding and, Jewish or not, I really think they only want their kids to be happy and to be able to share in their lives. I see that now. So write soon and let me know how the home front is, your job status, and are you still seeing that sweet young thing of last month? My bed is cold these days, but I have some great prospects!

Ciao Esther

P.S. Do you believe the dollar? I just might "have" to go to Europe this summer!

May 15, 1985

Dear Esther,

    I loved your letter. What a miracle about your dad and stepmom! It's funny you should mention parents because recently I've seen mine much more. As I grow older they seem to be more supportive. Or maybe I'm reinterpreting what I saw as nagging, negative comments in my direction. They still drive me crazy sometimes by ignoring me when I express feelings. They seem awkward, even between themselves, when dealing with real feelings. It's "Oh, it'll be alright, don't get worked up" or "Why don't you . . ." They can't just listen and comfort me. I guess I have to realize they may never be there for me as much as or in the way I want.

    As far as being out with them, I've never said it outright, but I haven't hidden anything, either. They know and again they tend to ignore it. The other day we were going to the community pool and I invited Dad to come in my car. He said, "Oh, what happens if you meet some boy there?" I said, "Probably not much!" Then my mother chimed in, "What happens if she meets a girl?" I said, somewhat shocked, "More possibly something!" Mom is more hip in that area and we've actually gotten closer since she's out working in the world and is more confident. Also, I'm no longer a threat of competition with Dad (he and I were always very close). He, on the other hand, doesn't quite know how to behave around me anymore and is more distant. I went to give him a hug the other day and he held me gingerly and slapped me on the back like a football player!

    Last week I did a brave thing and for the first time ever invited a lesbian friend to meet my parents at a Concert in the

Park. I was sweating bullets over what they were going to think of her and she of them. They got along great, particularly my father and she. They cracked jokes the whole time! My mother was a bit in a mood but she wasn't rude, which was what I was afraid of, and seemed to like my friend. I was relieved when it was over, but then realized maybe they didn't know she was gay (she didn't have a sign on her forehead or announce she was a card-carrying dyke), so did I really accomplish anything? If nothing else, for me at least, I brought together two previously separate areas of my life.

The gay issue is awkward for us, and I don't think they're ready to discuss it openly, since they can't even deal with other "charged" issues. And maybe, as you pointed out, I'm afraid of their disapproval as much as their fear of acknowledging it. Someday when our relationship is more solid I'll bring it up directly, but for now I'm just rebuilding from an antagonistic past with them and it's nice to have a working relationship.

So Esther, again congratulations on the active coming out to your parents. It must feel good. Your dad rivals mine for being a classic Jewish father, so there's hope for me yet!

That sweet young thing is out of my life, thank God! She wore out my feet and wallet fast, and there wasn't much under the surface, so I'm in your position—single and looking!

Good Hunting,

Ruth

May 21, 1976

Dear Sis,

Happy thirty-fifth birthday! One thing about being a twin, I never forget your birthday and I really miss you terribly, especially on such a big occasion! Mom and Dad are having a big wingding for me with the other six coming from around the state, and all the kids plus the aunts, uncles, etc. It'll actually be more of a reunion than my birthday party, but Mom loves to have everyone around and it will help fill the gap of your not being here.

Dammit Jeanie, I wish that whole business of your being a lesbian had never come up. Why did you have to say anything? You knew she'd pop her cork. None of us expected her and Dad (reluctantly) to disown you, though. You know how hard it's been for Dad and me never to mention your name? And she'd have a fit if she knew I was writing you. But I can't stand it, the horrible silence around you in the house. I have to be in contact with you if only to write, because you do exist and as "two peas in the pod," we can't ever be separated no matter what Mom and Dad say.

I must say I don't really understand your being "gay," your attraction to women. You really think it's a permanent thing, not just a phase? We both had crushes on teachers in grade school. Remember Miss Ames and the notes to Mrs. Taylor? But this is different. I've never felt sexually attracted to a woman. How did twins turn out so different? You're living with this woman named Pam in Chicago and you're happy? I hope so since you can never come home again and all. I don't feel Mom will ever soften up. She still is not talking to Aunt Helen and it's been ten years since that property line fight. I think she doesn't want your "perversion" to have anything to do with her, though I think she's afraid it does, and so the cutting off, the disownment. It's so strange to have you not be part of the family, even though among all of us kids we talk about you secretly. Dad is having a hard time "forgetting" you exist. He's aged a lot since the fracas last spring and is more withdrawn. I'm worried about him and his heart condition. Most of the farm work is done by Jeff and John and some farmhands now, but he still is up at 5:00 a.m. with the cows and works too hard. A month ago, when we were alone one night for a bit, he asked me if I'd heard from you. I said no and he shook his head sadly and went to bed. He misses you so much, Sis. You were his favorite. So Jeanie, I'd like to hear from you and stay in contact and I think Dad would love to know you are okay.

I want to come and visit you in the city because I miss talking to you terribly, you're my other half, but I don't know if that would be okay with your "friend" and besides, living at home again, I just can't. Someone's got to keep the peace with Mom. She's getting more willful every day and I have to look after Dad. Maybe sometime in the future I can make some excuse and sneak up to Chicago and we can catch up.

Again, I don't understand your lifestyle, but I hope you're happy. Don't be too angry with me or the rest. We just have to do what we have to do. Let's at least plan on celebrating our fortieth together! Write me at Karen's house. Happy Birthday twin!

I miss and love you,

Jeanie

July 3, 1985

Dear Leslie,

  It was great to see you and have *two* long chats on your last visit to your parents. I'm glad you got to see the boys before I trundle them off to camp. As your surrogate Mom (or really now your older friend), I like to keep in touch with your life, and I'm glad you haven't moved too far away. I find it hard to believe it's been 17 years since that inquisitive nine-year-old wandered into my young, married, and pregnant life in suburbia and our great friendship started with your "Can I babysit your baby when it's born?" You were always such a good child, but you obviously didn't have the most open relationship with your parents, so I tried my damndest to answer your questions and guide you as a friend and an adult. Being in my twenties while you were still at home, I don't know how wise I was, but we seemed to have helped each other over the tough spots through the years.

  Your latest announcement was a real shocker, and now that I've had time to think about it I'm afraid for you. Now don't get me wrong, I really don't think being a lesbian is wrong or sick. I love and accept you always. I do, however, find it strange to think of you as one, just because I always assumed you were straight and I have difficulty identifying with it as I've never had sexual feelings for women (what do they do?). At 26 you know your mind though, and if that's what is natural for you, then okay. And as a slightly maternal figure, I have to ask if your turning to women hasn't been because of the unsatisfying relationships you've had with men in the past and isn't there a chance you will go back to them? I'm not saying that in a condescending way, like "You're going through a phase," but frankly I'm worried that being gay will make your life more difficult and cause you more pain than if you were straight. There's a strong right-wing movement in this country now and gays are definitely not on its list of desirables. I'm afraid for you and what might happen.

Let me give you an example. Now you must keep this secret because I promised not to tell, but you remember Michelle, my other young friend from the neighborhood? Well, a year ago she too told me she was gay. (Now what does that say about my influence on young girls? Bizarre!) She told me a story about a lesbian friend of hers in college who was in bed with her Lebanese lover when the lover's mother and brother burst in and beat them up in a rage. The two of them quit college and moved to Los Angeles in fear of the family's anger.

I don't want something like that to happen to you. It's okay to come out to people like me, a diehard New York liberal, but please don't feel you have to tell everyone. The gossip around here, if it were known, would be fierce and damaging (probably more for your parents), and if your boss knew, you might lose your job. As mature as you've always been for your age, you are, in some ways, naive, so please be cautious about whom you tell and remember, some nasty people are out there.

One thing I forgot to tell you and you'll find amusing. Harry and I decided to see a play last summer, so we went to *Last Summer at Bluefish Cove* not knowing it was a lesbian play or a political benefit for Ginny Foat. We figured it out as soon as we walked in, though, with a crowd of almost all women couples, many of whom were sporting ties! Now Harry, an admitted chauvinist, and I enjoyed the play immensely, yet we felt very uncomfortable about being ignored by our seat mates and the ladies in general, as though we were invisible. We got an idea of what it must feel like to be a gay couple at a very straight affair! Sorry if I've been overly nagging or motherly about the whole lesbian issue, Leslie. It's just that I love you very much and don't want you to experience more pain than life already holds.

Harry and the boys and I are going to Tahoe when they return from camp and I can't wait to get out of the suburbs! The twins lost in the final round of Little League, but they'll survive. All three boys were glad to see you and I'm sure they send, as do I (with a huge hug), much, much love.

Take care, friend,

Molly

P.S. The apricot trees are groaning with fruit. You should come up and pick a bushel!

P.P.S. Are you sure men don't hold any interest for you?

July 17, 1985

Dear Molly,

Thanks for your wonderful letter! I greatly appreciated your sympathetic and nonjudgmental ear, as always and particularly this time, on my last visit to Mom and Dad. I haven't told them because they just wouldn't understand. Our relationship has never been that great as you know (they act as if I came from another planet), so why irritate them more? But you, you always were there to listen and bounce my feelings off of and I think you saved my childhood sanity. Thank you.

I was still scared to tell you about my sexuality because it is different, and I was a little afraid of some rejection. But you didn't reject me at all, thank God, and of course I do understand your concern. It's really very touching. I do think, though, your fear for me is blown out of proportion. Unfortunately, most of the country has those same fears. Don't you see that if I live my life in fear (in the closet), then I would create that same fear in others around me, not to mention that I would be as paranoid as hell. Fear and secretiveness are what keep homophobia alive and well in America. I refuse to live that way and I think my positive attitude is not naive, it's healthy. Of course I'm not going to tell everyone I run across I'm gay. It's not many people's (if anyone's) business what my sexuality is. And, people I care for and interact with closely I will tell, because I don't want to keep my love life separate from the rest my life.

I know all too well that violence is directed toward gays. I've had some pretty vicious catcalls from men, bordering on real confrontation, when I've walked down the street with my arm around Monica. But then I've had some pretty obscene comments yelled at me by straight construction workers as I'm walking alone downtown—some men will always be jerks. But I do believe we have to live openly (with common sense and discretion) for the whole consciousness to shift, and I do believe it will slowly shift with more exposure and knowledge between gay and straight people, not less. You fear my going through more pain than if I were straight. I'm not at all convinced of that. The way I see it, if I'm secure with who I am, then if someone gets weird with my lesbianism (no one so far), that's more their problem than mine. I would support them in changing their viewpoint, but not take on their negative energy if it persisted. I won't say I'll never feel pain related to homosexuality, but it's not the sexual preference itself causing it, it's the fearful minds of people. Everything I've encountered in my relationships with women is the same stuff I had with men. Molly, there really is no difference, and pain is a part of everyone's life. Ours just appears different.

As to your plaintive questions about men and me. No, I haven't written them off forever and in fact I had a very brief affair with a very straight businessman last fall, but for the most part it is women I notice and feel strongly about in an intimate way. Being with a woman is just so much more intense, exciting, and alive for me (I know you find that hard to relate to but it's true) that I can't ever see going back to a heterosexual lifestyle. As for what we "do" in bed—Molly, use that vivid imagination of yours, remembering another woman knows what you're feeling physically, and probably emotionally, much more accurately than a man can. There's no comparison for me. Maybe bisexual is a more accurate term for me and my main interest is definitely women, so I have no problem being a lesbian. So I appreciate your concern, but please DON'T WORRY about me! I'm healthy and happy and growing in many directions (unfortunately too much in the waistline as well). I am getting bored with my bookkeeping job and want to branch out into something more creative, but that will come in time when I have saved some money. In the meantime, Monica and I are getting along fine, growing closer, and we're looking for a Siamese cat! My next visit I want to bring her along so you can meet her (I don't know about my parents, though). She's a sweetie.

It was so good to see you and the boys. God, they've grown fast. Give them and Harry my love. That was hysterical about the play! I wish I could have been there to see your faces! You know I love apricots and I'd love to come get some, but I just can't get away until next month for the 80 miles north to you. Make me some jam!

Love you,
Leslie

P.S. Don't worry!

P.P.S. Thanks for understanding. It means a lot!

Chapter III
ABOUT THE CHILDREN

DO WE TELL THE CHILDREN?

June 9, 1970

Dear Amy,

It was good to see you after what seems like eons since we last spent time in Philadelphia together. A little different lifestyle here in the country of Sonoma, eh? It suits Allie and me and our artistic temperaments to have all this land and freedom, and my kids love it here. The only drawback I feel sometimes is a lack of community with other lesbians. Sometimes I would like some more everyday support and contact with them. That's what made your visit so very special, catching up with the current issues of our minority and remembering we aren't the only ones way out here.

One issue that I didn't bring up with you, I would like to discuss now, for it is something difficult for Allie and me to get a perspective on, and I trust your judgment. Basically it's: Do we come out to the kids or not? We've been battling the pros and cons now for a long time, most of the seven years we've been together. It is particularly pressing now for I'm afraid Brian thinks I hate men, especially since he sees his father more often now, and we all know how I feel about him. I really don't want to convey that message, but then we don't have many men over and I think he's wondering about it. Maybe at thirteen he needs more male influence (though Allie and I do all the active things a man would do), but how do we arrange it? And Terri is just entering puberty now and I find her looking at us questioningly sometimes when Allie and I express affection. (We are very careful not to overdo it in front of them.) We're scared to death at the consequences of telling them. First of all, would they understand the concept of two women loving each other as a man and a woman do? Would they accept our relationship even if it meant incurring the shame of their friends? We're afraid they'd be really upset and not trust us after that, as much as they love us, me as their mother and Allie as their pal. Would they feel they would have to be gay, too?

I found Terri in the bathroom the other day applying an old pink lipstick of mine. It was hard not to laugh as I told her how beautiful she looked. And Brian does the most incredible feats of daring on the lake when the O'Shaughnessy girls are there (double flips that make my heart stop). It seems only a matter of days until the first date. At these crucial years of awakening sexuality we're afraid of damaging their identities and/or choices about it. On the other hand, my kids are not dumb (am I bragging?), so despite the potential crises, wouldn't it be easier to come clean and explain our life together? We just don't know. We feel we're damned if we do and damned if we don't. We lead a perfectly normal life out here on our 14 acres, they go to school, and have great friends, we do everything together—but the reality is, we are abnormal according to society. That's the bitch, and Allie and I just don't know what to do.

If we come out, I'm afraid Steve, who I think must have some suspicions anyway, will turn my sweet Brian and Terri against me with homophobic crap. I don't know if they are old enough to resist such pressure and I'm really terrified of Steve's using it to try to get custody of them. That would devastate me and tear up the kids.

I thought you, being a teacher, could give us some valuable input in making a decision. You deal with kids every day and even though you're not "out" at school, you probably would have more of an idea of the consequences. Allie and I are really torn with the issue and would love to hear what you have to say.

I hope your delicate situation at home with Mary has cleared up and that things are going smoothly again and summer school started well. It was good you got away from the whole big city scene for a while. I miss it intellectually sometimes, but our little "back-forty" here is, as you saw, perfect for us now. By the way, my sculpture now has an exquisite left breast to match the other. On to the belly! And our garden! Allie and I are delighted with the progress of our peas, and our corn is almost a foot and a half high! Come back in August for the fruits of our loving labor. Give my best to the gang, especially Stephanie, and maybe next year I'll make it East with my gal. Again, it was *wonderful* to have you for a whole week. I miss you terribly already!

Much Sonoma love,

BETH

Oct. 31, 1984

Dear Mom and Dad,

Happy Halloween! It was good to talk to you last Sunday and catch up on all the Missoula gossip. Glad to hear Trudy is still happily married after a whole three months and Fred has landed his first grown-up job! At 31 I'm beginning to feel old looking at the "kids" doing adult things. It's funny how life speeds up after 20 and turns out much differently than we figured at 18. Case in point, me, who thought I wanted to be a forest ranger and settle down and have 10 kids (with another ranger of course), and who turned out to be a fairly successful graphic artist/lesbian in a major city. You really have been wonderful supporting me through all my changes and in particular, accepting my being gay and my life partner Joy into the family. It has meant the world to me to share openly with you about my relationship with her. And now I have another big one to drop in your lap that I just couldn't bring up on the phone, and especially since we are coming at Christmas, it must be told. So get a stiff drink and sit down and here goes!

Even as the vision of my life at 18 turned out much differently than I pictured, I did "settle down" with Joy in our wonderful equivalent of marriage—five years this December! You have seen our happiness and commitment to each other. Another part of that 18-year-old's vision also stuck with me—wanting children. And for the most part, I dismissed that as not possible being with a woman, even though Joy also shared a love of kids, yet the desire never quite faded. And last January we heard about a conference to be held in San Francisco called Lesbians Choosing Children and we looked at each other and immediately decided to go.

The conference blew our minds. There were lots of women who had had children by donor insemination. Some had chosen a known donor and some had chosen an unknown donor, going to a sperm bank and being inseminated by a doctor. Most of the women at the conference were like us, finding out the possibilities. There were doctors, lawyers, and therapists to answer and discuss the myriad of questions about all the things that come up around two women having a child. We were ecstatic since we knew deep down that we wanted children, a family, and indeed it would be difficult but certainly not impossible. We gathered up all the information and talked about it seriously for six months solid. We agreed I would have the first child and Joy the second in a few years.

At this point, Mom and Dad, we were torn, because we really wanted to tell you and Joy's parents, to explain, and have you on our side. But frankly we were afraid of a heavy-duty reaction (the baby not having a father) and a lot of confusion and emotion interfering with our decision. So we went ahead secretively (just telling two friends) and drew up a legal contract spelling out our commitment to each other emotionally and financially with respect to our family-to-be. The process really strengthened our union. We began the arduous process of picking an unknown donor at the sperm bank, and my being "seeded" during my fertile times. It was a pain, but not too bad, considering the potential result. We had considered a friend donating his sperm so we would know who else had created the baby, but there would be lots of potential legal complications (if he later wanted actively to parent) and we didn't want to have interference with our family of the future, it was to be our baby, and so chose the rather impersonal unknown donor.

This is rather a long-winded way of telling you the thrilling, if somewhat shocking, news that you will be grand-parents on or about May 15, 1985! I got pregnant after only two months (most women take 6–8 months of trying before concep-tion) and I am two and a half months "gone." I now feel so special and warm and excited. The other part of my vision has come true. Now, of course, I want to share our happiness and creation with you.

I know you're most likely upset by the fact there will be no father (though we will have plenty of male friends around). You probably have lots of questions like: How can two women raise a normally adjusted child? What about the community? Is it fair to the child to grow up in a fatherless and potentially controversial environment? We have looked seriously at these questions and after talking to many lesbian mothers, we saw no drastic difference in their children's mental and emotional adjustment. Many, many families today are single-parent, and those kids make it all right, even through messy divorces. The main question to us is "What is a family?" And as far as Joy and I can see, it is a unit of related people who love and nurture one another and declare themselves family. Certainly, both Joy and I have very positive models in our respective families and we want to re-create that with our child, to have him/her loved by grandparents, aunts, uncles, the whole nine yards. The only difference is that there is no dad. And certainly there may be problems when the child grows up and asks questions, but we feel strong enough that with the truth he/she will be resilient and will accept the way it is.

Obviously there is much to discuss with you in the coming

months (years) about this, and Joy and I both hope you understand why we didn't tell you beforehand. Remember that it is our
love for each other, just as it was between the two of you, that
created this life and will support it in its miraculous unfolding.

I remain your loving daughter,

Theresa

Nov. 8, 1984

Dear Theresa,

Your father and I had three stiff drinks with your letter and we're still in shock two days later! You're actually pregnant? We had assumed there was no possibility of your ever having a baby except if you changed your mind and found a man, and so we were settled with the fact you are a lesbian, and no children. But to have a baby with Joy by artificial insemination?

We understand you are pregnant out of a strong desire to have a family and knowing the fullness that children add to life, we understand that desire. We do, however, question whether you are fully prepared to deal with the consequences of an unconventional family, given your relationship with Joy. We are obviously unfamiliar with a two-mother family and just have never given thought to an option we didn't know existed. Frankly it is shocking the idea of an unknown man's sperm being injected into you, and you and Joy raising this half-mystery baby with no father. If it's a boy or a girl, what or who will be the male role model? As much as you two love each other, a child should have some male figure to identify with and learn from. Have you truly considered this, the absence of close knowledge of half the human race? Would the child's sexuality be affected by two lesbian mothers? What if the child wants to know who his/her father is at age 12 or whenever? How would it be for the child if friends asked about his/her father and he/she didn't have one? We are concerned, Theresa, that your child would have more than the usual burdens of childhood and might suffer from them. We have no doubt you and Joy will make excellent parents and can cope with the usual traumas, but are you ready for things you might not anticipate, having created this life? Raising a child is a great responsibility as well as a great joy and we just wonder if you are prepared for the repercussions of an unusual family.

We do realize that children are resilient and there are many single mothers and unusual family combinations these days, but there is usually a father or father figure somewhere about for the child to relate to. We are concerned about the gap which by nature you and Joy can't possibly fill. Of course, being that you have gone ahead in your usual, forceful way (we were hurt at not being consulted beforehand on such an important issue) and you do intend to raise your children, we will support you as best we can. We are still having a hard time with the idea of being grandparents to a child from an unlikely source, but of course we will accept the child as he/she will need all the love possible. Trudy and Fred are startled also. They figured they would provide the grandchildren. And, in fact, Trudy and new son-in-law Howard are very upset that you are going to have a baby by artificial insemination. Remember, Howard's father is a minister and Trudy has gotten very religious especially since the wedding (which has surprised us because she was such an atheist as a teenager). We've tried to calm them down, but I warn you, they may give you a very hard time. They feel very strongly against the idea. And your grandparents! We haven't told them because they barely comprehend your sexuality. This would send them into a tailspin. That announcement, my darling daughter, we will leave to you! It will probably not be easy to explain a virgin birth and we hope you figure out a way to tell them so they aren't upset and will accept the child.

As you said, there is a lot to talk about concerning your "delicate condition." We will call you soon, and at Christmas we all can discuss our future family. At this point we are truly ambivalent, confused by emotions and thoughts and questions. But the important thing is providing your child with the best possible environment in which to grow up. Knowing your and Joy's capacity for love, we are not concerned about that basic ingredient of a family and life itself. We *are* concerned, however, about the two of you dealing with the "real world."

Dear amazing daughter we send

Much confused love to you and Joy,

M+D

P.S. We assume Joy has told her parents. We want to call them to see how they feel about your news and commiserate.

ABOUT THE CHILDREN

YOU'VE GONE TOO FAR

Nov. 11, 1984

Dear Theresa,

You've always had nerve and been the eccentric in the family, but this time you've gone too far. I've never been totally comfortable with the idea of homosexuality, but over the years I got used to you and Joy. You seemed to have a genuine affection for each other and Mom and Dad accepted that. But having a child by artificial insemination is sick and an abomination before God! Howard and I are appalled that you would even think for a second you could raise a child without a father and the sacrament of marriage. Children are supposed to be a product of love between a man and a woman, not something you go to the sperm bank for and raise with your lesbian lover! Theresa, wake up, this is not a fantasy, this is one of God's creations in the real world! Your child would have no father and be horribly warped and unbalanced as he grew up. A woman just can't replace a man in the family unit, and a child growing up with two lesbians, God knows how he'd turn out.

Howard and I talked to his father, who, as you know, is a minister. He was deeply shocked and suggested strongly that we urge you to give the baby up for adoption at birth. He knows of a good adoption agency here in Missoula and you could come and have the baby here and be assured it was adopted by a good family.

I know I'm your baby sister, but please listen and wake up from your kinky California dream and consider the child. He would never be accepted by other children and be set apart by not having a father. A child needs a dad. Can you imagine our childhood without Dad having been there to help us out and love us? How do you think Fred, star quarterback and weightlifter in school, would have turned out with two moms?

Howard and I are repulsed you have even thought of it, never mind gone ahead. And you've hurt Mom and Dad very much by not consulting with them beforehand. You are really very thoughtless. And the idea of an anonymous man's sperm being used is really ungodly and cold. You are taking God's miracle of life and twisting it to your selfish purposes. If you want a child we suggest you straighten up and find a good man to have a family with or just be content with Joy. The two don't mix. You have really gone too far, Theresa, and though Mom and Dad don't seem as outraged, they are very confused. So for God's sake consider the position you've put them in. They probably won't force the adoption issue on you, but please see that is the only right thing to do. Don't fly in the face of God's Will!

I will make an appointment with Rev. Whiteley for Christmas. Please listen to him and to your own conscience.

Your sister,

Trudy

Nov. 15, 1984

Dear Trudy,

Frankly I was shocked and hurt by your attitude toward my having a baby. Where does all that righteous religious stuff come from—you who snuck out of Sunday school as often as you went and stopped going to church at all at 13? It sounds as if you've adopted Howard's (and his father's) dogma lock, stock, and barrel, and honestly, this "born again" disdain does not become you, little sister.

I know we've never been very close, but I thought you supported me in my, albeit, unusual choices. I didn't expect you to be overjoyed, but I think Howard has warped your judgment on this. You know damn well I've always wanted a child, so what's so strange and perverted about my having one? Joy and I certainly have not done it on a lark or without knowing the difficulties ahead. We expected a furor about our announcement, but, as when we came out, we expected your support and understanding for the love Joy and I obviously have, to prevail over the differences. This "abomination" garbage is really quite disturbing to both Joy and me. I have never felt so satisfied and happy as now being pregnant and looking forward to our new family life and you want me to give the baby up for adoption? No way, Trudy. I don't even want to see Rev. Whiteley when I come home and I have my doubts about seeing Howard or even you, if your attitude doesn't change.

Joy and I don't go to church per se, but we certainly believe in God, or a Higher Spirit, or whatever you want to call the Oneness of All. God doesn't just belong to white, nuclear, middle class Christian families. He/She is there for all of us. God is the quality of being in relation to the Whole and does not judge, especially in the way you expressed. We have as loving a relationship as anyone has and lead healthy productive lives. With our strong desire for children, why shouldn't we have them? God knows, a lot of children I've seen are brought up in the unhappy, unloving environment of a sour or broken marriage, and they suffer terribly. Our "marriage" is very strong and loving, and we feel even without a father and the difficulties that that may entail (mostly with society we feel, not with the child and us), our family environment will be healthy, honest, and supportive of the children's growth.

As much as I love and respect Dad, a father is not a sacred being, and I don't think it's crucial that there is a male figure or father for a child. We have many male friends, straight and gay, and we see our children choosing their male characteristics from a variety of examples. Children after all are not carbon copies of their same sex parent (look at us in respect to Mom), and are influenced by many people growing up. That is why we are certain that having two mothers will not be detrimental to our kids innately. The only problem we really see is society's reaction to our extraordinary family, but we hope that with our support, a sympathetic community having like families, and growing awareness about such families in the larger community, the child's difference will be minimal. After all, most kids feel different in some way or another.

I am saying all this so that perhaps you will relax a little and understand our motives. We don't need to justify or explain because we are clear on our choice and path. God doesn't make mistakes, and we are humbled by the miracle we have been given.

Please, please Trudy, let go of the patriarchal religious fervor for a moment and remember I am your sister, I love you, and my child will want to know his/her aunt. I ask you not to condone necessarily, but to accept my family-to-be. If you don't, I would be very saddened.

Love,

Theresa

You are the first together
                    I have known,
        releasing
                heaven and
                        hell
                            in me as
        I pour my chest of jewels and cobwebs
                                        into the daylight
                                                of us.

I am awkward
            with your
        gifts,
                for all I feel
                        is the gift
                            of you.

I am inspired and
                humbled
                        by your stance in life,
        it is powerful and
                    lined with the
                            tenderness of a woman.

I love you
            woman,
        I yield and
                together
                    I stand with you
                                    in awe.

Chapter IV
LESBIAN RELATIONSHIPS

MY DEAREST WOMAN

April 17, 1983

My dearest woman,

I have been in Paris now 48 hours, and as excited as I am about being in this magical city and delivering my paper in two days, I greatly miss your physical presence. After 20 years you'd think I'd be starved for an exotic vacation apart from you (granted, with some work involved). There have been so few times we've been separated for more than a few days. But when I saw Notre Dame and the Seine again yesterday, all I wanted was to have you by my side to share my delight and expand on our second honeymoon. Paris is somehow empty without a lover and you are my eternal lover, mate, comfort, and inspiration. I don't feel depressed or stranded without you. I just feel like a part of me is missing, as if my reflection in the mirror were gone. Our phone conversation was great, but you were way over there and I couldn't hold you or kiss you good-night. Sigh!

This is the first time I've really had to write between bouts of jet lag, a quick sightseeing walk, and endless shop talks with my colleagues from around the world. The conference started this morning and is proving to be quite controversial. There is a not-so-subtle war going on between the "old-boy" therapists and the "new gang" of free-form, mostly American therapists. The hornet's nest is buzzing and I can't wait to deliver my bombshell on Wednesday. Is the psychotherapist world *really* ready to accept homosexuality as natural with my theory that the male/female balance in all of us more truly determines our attractions and compatibilities than society or our sex do? We'll see, my sweet. Thank God I've got a few pals here who respect my work. Remember Hendrick Holliger and Betty Thurber? They're here.

Wish me a strong stomach and a clear voice, for I really want everyone to hear my paper and be moved, both logically and emotionally.

I wish you could have come to hear me in my shining hour, but I do understand that between your big project this week and your uncle in the hospital, you can't. I do hope, though, you can manage to take off next week and join me. I know I can't count on it but it sure would be heaven. We could go anywhere in Europe! It's been six years since our last continental fling and I wouldn't mind sharing a Sacher torte in Vienna (remember those huge pillows at the Sacher Hotel? Mmm . . .), or a gelato and gondola ride in Venice by moonlight, or . . . . Sorry, I'm getting carried away as usual. If you make it or not we must plan a big trip this fall, obligations and our very important careers be damned. I adore traveling with you, anywhere, and we haven't done enough of it lately. That's why it seems so strange not to have you here in my big, comfy, empty bed!

How can I possibly love you so much after all this time? I must need a shrink! It just gets deeper and better and more vastly rich, my life with you. We seem to breathe together without getting smothered. We push each other to our highest selves without nagging, and though we often don't spend much time together, an immeasurable bond of trust and love always makes our moments together sparkle. Our growth individually and together has been beyond my wildest imagination. When I look back on those painful coming-out years and struggling with school, I never could have imagined that one spilt drink could have transformed all of that into such a union. You, my darling, have shown me my power and my vulnerability, and have been right by my side as I have soared to great professional heights and heights of self-knowledge. You are so very precious to me, my heart, and it sometimes takes being away from you for me to fully appreciate that and express how utterly I love you. It must be this city, or the water, for I am a big mush ball right now, tearing away, but I actually do feel you here so I will sleep with your spirit.

Between now and Wednesday I'd better get my therapist persona together. They wouldn't listen to a weepy (stereotypical) woman and yet I will sneakily hit them in the ole female side. Can't wait! Sleep well, love. I hope your uncle is better and your project gets done and accepted and you come to me. I miss you fiercely and hold you in my heart always.

Yours,
Rachael

P.S. Remember to take Xerxes to have her shots on the 23rd and give her a head rub for me!

MY VIRGO

I awoke with you &
                    found
           the falling virgin moon
                              in my arms.

Moontide
           had swept you
                         home
           on wakening,
                         leaving its silvery
      foam on my limbs,
                      they shiver
                                against
                                     the ebb.

FRUIT

Watching you
           slowly suck
                      ripe plums,
tongue buried
           in livid meat,
           juice leaving your lips
                              heady, wet,
                                        red–
           I meet your eyes
      and ripen quickly.

March 27, 1982

Dear Jane,

    I don't know any easy way of saying this, so I'll just be up front and say it's over with us, at least as lovers. I just can't reconcile the strain and drain we both have put up with over the last five months and I can't see any change in the future that wouldn't compromise either or both of us, so let's call it quits with no regrets.

    Please don't take this too personally. There's nothing wrong with you. We are just two very different types of people and even though we complement each other in many ways, we also seem to upset each other a lot. So it's best we stop now rather than drag it on, much as we love each other. Love, and our differing degrees of it, seemed to be the major issue since our blowup last October, the fact you were in love with me and I was not in love with you. I really wasn't lying the whole time and it wasn't as if I didn't thoroughly enjoy our wonderful, intimate time together. It's just my feelings never matured to the in love place and there's no "reason" for that. But if it's not there I can't fake it, and, as you say, you deserve someone who adores you. I truly hope you find that someone.

    As you have noticed I am very independent and maybe I am resisting a relationship in general, resistant to receiving, but believe me I tried my damndest to make it work. I just can't change significantly enough to fit your picture, so we must go different directions as lovers. I am incredibly sad in making this choice. It's not cavalier or easy on my part to let go of our loving intimacy. I've gotten accustomed to our closeness. I realize this will hurt you and I apologize for that. I fear your going away, but I think you knew on some level it wasn't working and that this is best. I hope you will see that now or later.

What I want is for us to let go of the form we created and let our love lead us into the most natural way of being with each other. I realize you may be upset, angry, hurt and not want to see me for a while, but please don't throw the "baby out with the bathwater." We've shared too much over the last year to chuck it all, and I most dearly want a relationship of love and support with you throughout our lives, but not as lovers. Maybe you can only be with me as a lover. If so, I would be very sad, but would understand. But please be open to the possibility of our relationship becoming even fuller on another level. I know the phrase "let's be friends" is infuriating, but for me friendship is a very high level of love and trust, perhaps the highest, and I want that. Please trust me that this is right for both of us, even though it is I who is initiating it.

Your radiant smile is always in my heart now. You gave me many gifts, the full moon on the waves off the pier, your patience and support of me and my personal growth, and the thoughts, dreams, and truth of yourself. And the most precious was your love which I learned to receive most gratefully and humbly, and which I will always treasure. I gave you all I was able and I am sad it just wasn't enough to bridge the gap between us.

I am sorry to write this, but I didn't trust myself to be able to express it all in person fully, or you to hear it without closing down. Please don't bolt. I'm not rejecting you as a person, just letting go of you as a long-term lover. There is a clear distinction.

I love you more than you know, Jennifer

April 30, 1980

Dear Laurel,

Greetings from sunny California! Hope the late snows of Colorado haven't slowed you down too much. The fog is starting its summer dance early here, but in general the weather is gorgeous. I'm writing you for personal therapy and because I need some solid advice. You are the most stable person I know (by that I don't mean boring), so I thought I would run my latest Dyke Drama by you.

It's actually the incestuous (and there's an unintentional pun in here) and seemingly common Dyke Dilemma. The usual: a couple have been together for years, one dries up sexually, and the other seeks relief with another (usually a friend of both), while maintaining the first (love) relationship. As you recall, I was the one to seek relief when I was with Linda, enduring all the jealousies, hassles, and trips that went on for years. Now, as of last night, I'm in the "another" role and it's extremely uncomfortable. And you'll never guess whom I'm having an affair with—my friend/employer Marilyn's lover, Kate. Let me back up a bit.

I first met Marilyn in a bar late one night and we danced up a storm. She didn't seem to be with anyone, so I was interested and told her so. She was coy at first, but by closing we made a date for the following weekend. Again we danced all night and had great fun (and a few intense kisses), but she went home alone despite my urging to do otherwise. The next day she called me up and offered me a job at her printing shop. I jumped at it for I was unemployed at the time. After a week I began to get the picture. She had a lover, Kate. So I slowed down my interest in Marilyn, especially since I was now working for her, but she kept asking me to go dancing, to movies, etc. We had fun, but I felt strange, wondering about this mysterious Kate. Eventually I met her at a party at their home and liked her a lot. Marilyn and I would still go out and party often after work with lots of other women (never with Kate), but occasionally the three of us would do something together.

One night the three of us were going to have dinner at a restaurant. Kate and I showed up, but Marilyn called saying she had an emergency at the office and she'd meet us at their house. It was the first time Kate and I had been alone and we had a delightful evening getting to know each other much better. Kate talked about her background in New York, her teaching career in philosophy, and a little about her bizarre relationship with Marilyn. She seemed tolerant of Marilyn's behavior (they'd been together for four years), but there was an underlying sadness, so I didn't press it. Anyway, we went back to the apartment and still no Marilyn, so we had some more drinks and spirited talk. I was finding myself attracted to her and it was getting late, so I got up to leave. At the door there was a hesitation and silently we kissed. I was buzzing for days and terrified of what we had done. I didn't see Kate for a couple of weeks after that and tried to be cool around Marilyn. But the next time I saw her at the office there was a storm of sexual energy around us. I was wild, for I don't like to have anything to do with "married" women as a rule, but Kate had me really going.

I left the ball in her court and the inevitable happened. She asked me out to a movie and afterward, we went back to my place and we couldn't help ourselves—we made beautiful, passionate love. We felt elated and very guilty at the same time. Kate said she and Marilyn hadn't had sex in six months and she had been going berserk as a result. Marilyn had some sort of problem with it, probably stemming from early incest traumas with her father. Kate said she has been very sympathetic and loves Marilyn very much, but that she has her own needs and had begun to feel rejected and undesirable herself.

Now, Laurel, I'm not looking for a "Relationship," but I certainly enjoyed being intimate with Kate and want to continue it, even if it eventually costs me my job and friendship with Marilyn. We agreed last night to keep it a secret because Marilyn, even though she plays around, is intensely jealous. I really don't want to bust up their relationship and I figure if Kate is willing to have an affair, I will go with that and try to keep everything separate. I really feel uncomfortable because Marilyn has been so good to me and I hate being in the middle of a triangle from any angle, but the energy between Kate and me is so magical. What do I do?

Please give me your feedback. You've known me for 10 years and I'm in a real quandary, again dammit. Don't think I purposely go out looking for these situations! The lesbian world is full of them. Why I wonder?

Hope your business is doing well. Give Jane a hug, not to mention Rudolph, Sylvester, Indira, and all the other strays you might have there. And the biggest hug to you, my friend.

Your dyke drama queen,

Carolyn

May 8, 1980

Dear Isabelle,

Greetings and salutations! Good news, I'll probably be wafting into the steamy deserted island of Manhattan sometime in August. Are you ready for a West Coast refugee? Much as I love my life here in California, I am often starved for the theater, the galleries, the acid wit and gossip of the Big Apple. S.F. is fine, but a shadow of the cultural inferno of N.Y.C. I miss it and I miss you.

I'm almost done with the term at State and a good thing. I'm exhausted after getting up at 6:00 a.m. for months and dealing with heady term papers at night and on weekends. Added to that has been the emotional drain in my relationship with Marilyn. We don't seem to be getting anywhere, and in fact are quarreling more. I've tried to be patient and to talk about the incest issue, which seems to be behind her lack of interest in sex with me. But we only get to a certain point and she gets threatened somehow and then aggressive and then I get upset and on it goes. It usually ends up with her marching out the door and coming back late at night. We always make up, but the underlying tension is getting to me.

Last week I broke the sexual tension for myself, but added to it with Marilyn. I started another affair. I had to, for I was beginning to chew up my self-esteem. It's extremely dangerous and I feel loaded with guilt because, like my brief stormy affair with Kit last year, it is someone Marilyn knows, and indeed is an employee of hers as well as a friend. Her name is Carolyn and she's an attractive, bright woman who is part of Marilyn's entourage and whom I got to know over the last few months. I really didn't plan anything, but an attraction started on both sides and last week we got together and had a sexual explosion. It was fabulous, hot, and long overdue. We were both a bit freaked out by the intensity of it and the guilt that surrounds it. We agreed to keep it secret from Marilyn. If she was so upset last year, God knows what would happen if she knew about Carolyn. And I'm particularly concerned because Marilyn has said she was thinking about seeing a therapist to resolve the incest issue, and I don't want anything to impede her trying to work out this incredible burden on her psyche. I love her so much and want her so much to be happy, to not feel driven to go out to the bars and have one nighters (which I know she does). She comes back exhausted, looking for affection from me, but is incapable of sexual expression. That childlike, frightened look really gets to me, and I want to go find her father and slit his throat for what he did to her from age four on. It's really tragic what that's done to her life and she can't seem let go of it and forgive herself for something her bastard father did before she could barely talk.

So the timing of this affair is horrible, and I hate separating my sex life from my love life, but I have to do it for my own self-worth. Carolyn makes me feel desirable, exciting, and alive again after a long period of shutting down. I've made it clear to Carolyn of my priority with Marilyn and she accepts that. I hope we can keep that emotional distance and keep it under wraps for a while at least. I feel like I'm juggling 10 balls at once, and I just hope I can keep them all in the air!

Oh Isabelle, I can't wait to visit you and be in my old sane/insane environs of the Village and blast out some of this wild drama into the streets and lofts of dear N.Y.C.! I need a break and I need the company of old friends.

I'll be in touch soon about the dates, and so on. Give my love to the ladies at the Duchess! Write me your news, loves, real life in the real city. Oh, the angst of life!

Love,

Kate

June 12, 1980

Dear Mary,

I've been working so hard at keeping my business growing
that I've had no time to respond to your wonderful letter. But it's
late at night and I need to keep up with you for my sanity's sake
and to let you know I miss you. Your new love sounds wonderful,
just what you wanted and needed after dear nutty Patsy. (Didn't
you see when she was with me how schitzy she was?) Anyway,
congratulations! It seems so long ago when we worked that
horrible nightshift together down in Auburn and terrorized the
town topless during the day. I can't see why you have stayed there
in that small town way of life, but then I find myself missing the
deep forests, the rivers, and the mountains, so I may go out there
to visit you while Kate is back East in August. Sound good?

I don't want to see the family, though. It's still too difficult.
I've started seeing a therapist to deal with Dad and the whole
thing. It's excruciating and I've said I was going to quit a thousand
times since the first session, but between Sheila, my therapist,
and Kate, I've hung in there. It's amazing what horrors I've
dredged up that I tried hard to forget, but I have to. My relationship with Kate was getting very tense and I was so unhappy with
myself. It is so hard, though, to begin the process of letting go of
the guilt and the feelings of fear and anger not only with Dad but
also with the whole family. It's so complex and so painful, and
sometimes I wonder if I've ever been happy. It's like poison in my
bloodstream. Will I ever purge myself of its presence?

I will lose Kate, though, if I can't break through. I've been
impotent now for a long time with her. I seem to be able to have
sex only with acquaintances or complete strangers and blow off

the rest by dancing. She had an affair with a friend of mine last year, which nearly drove me insane with jealousy, bringing up all the old fears and terrors. It didn't last long, but I'm afraid she will go out again and find someone else to satisfy her if I can't. I wouldn't blame her logically, but the idea of her in bed with someone else drives me mad. I'm still hanging onto her betrayal last year with Kit. God that hurt and it's been stormy ever since.

I love Kate so much, though. She's such a fine person and patient with all my wildness, so I'm sticking to the therapy, tough as it is. Sheila says it's not at all uncommon for lesbians and gays to be victims of incest and in fact recommended that I join a group over in the East Bay that is forming specifically for gay victims. I don't know about that yet, maybe in a few months or so. All I know is I want me back, I want to discover who I am in this morass of my life, to live presently and happily with Kate, and to stop running away from the snake that's gripped me for so long.

Sorry, Mary, for getting so heavy. You are one of few people who knows my past and since it's up for scrutiny, I needed to talk with someone close who is outside my current environment. I'm really eager to see you and meet your new girlfriend, and catch up on the three years we haven't seen each other. Thanks for your letters, they really have meant a lot to me, and again, sorry for being such a lousy correspondent. How does the second week in August sound? See you soon!

Much love,

Marilyn

Jan. 28, 1982

Dear June,

I still can't believe it. Even after a month I'm more
confused and just crazy, hurt, and angry that Lynne left me for a
man. How could she do that after seven years together? And she
had been screwing him for three months while my father was
dying! I was in enough pain already. How could she have done
that, especially then? The two most important people in my life
just went away, abandoning me. One of them would have been
enough, but then I would have had the other. I have less than
nothing now. I have betrayal and it's eating a bitter hole in me.

I really miss my father, he was my pal as you know, the
sweetest old guy who ever ate feta cheese. We were always tight,
a special bond, and I took care of him for the last five months,
completely, whatever it took. I was often terribly drained, but I
was really there for him until the end. He never liked hospital
food, so I made sure he got his dolmas and feta, some *real* food. I
was really close to him always, "his Annie," and I thought I was as
close to Lynne.

When I think I came home exhausted from the hospital
while she was with John, my stomach turns. It would have been
equally devastating if she had been seeing a woman. But after all
this time to want to be with a man. There's nothing I can do, I'm
helpless. I'm not a man and that's apparently what she wants.
Goddamn it, we had a seven-year marriage, how could she chuck
it all for a man she's not even in love with? She just wants to
screw him and that's like a knife in my love for her, in our love for
each other.

I really hate her for it because she never told me she had

desires to be with men again. Yes, she said vaguely a year and a half ago that she felt some desire to be with men, but she never TOLD me, as if it were a serious thing that she would probably act on. So she hid it away rather than talk about it, and eventually she snuck it in and sprung it on me, already done. Of course I would have been upset at any time, but to hide it and then do it secretly just hurts so much.

And as if that wasn't enough, she "WANTS TO BE FRIENDS!" She actually wanted me to be her "special" friend and to be over there often. She somehow imagined I would forgive and forget she screwed him the night before in the same bed and house we shared for seven years. Do you believe that? No way! I don't trust her anymore. She can't have her cake and eat it too, not with me. She's made her choice and I wouldn't put up with less than the love we started out with and I thought we had. I can't begin to tell you how hurt and empty I am without her, especially without my Dad.

And June, I even feel betrayed by our friends who still see her, as if nothing happened. How can they not feel outraged? How can they ignore that she pushed me out for a man and socialize with her as if I never existed? I'm mad and hurt, and feel betrayed by them, too.

So, June, I'm lost and alone. I've gone out dancing a few times, but I have zero interest in anyone really. I feel like an open wound and I can't imagine healing, even with time. Thank God my job has kept me very busy. I would have gone insane without it. I told my boss she couldn't fire me, at least not this year. I wish you were here to be with me. When you and I split up it was a natural thing, a little painful, but we stayed close and our love didn't change. We just stopped being lovers. But this is like my right arm deciding to leave and be on someone else. I loved her more than any man ever could. We had a wonderful life together, or so I thought. Now there's just a sharp pain where she was.

Enough of my problems. How's everything in dear old Gary? Are your parents still living in the old neighborhood? Write me soon, babe, and let me know what you're up to. Your love life has got to be better than mine!

All love,

Anna

LESBIAN RELATIONSHIPS

MUSEUM NOTES

Journal
Sept. 30, 1974

Had the most extraordinary encounter today at the
museum. Went there with Robert for the much-anticipated Hittite
show. We split up as usual and I started salivating over the
exquisite gold and iron artifacts from that ancient Turkish culture.
The delicate reindeer with their noble antlers particularly
enthralled me, calling up a picture of a sensitive people who
respected these creatures and interacted with Nature in a sacred
way.

I was entranced, looking down on a case of miniature
reindeer, when I was pulled by someone else's energy opposite
me. I looked up and saw a pair of large, sable-brown eyes which I
fell into. We were locked together, a very elemental energy, like
that of the art beneath us, passing between us. We were known to
each other—inexplicably. The moment seemed forever and yet
was perhaps a few seconds of real time before her parents joined
her and reclaimed their charge. They moved her off quickly and it
was only then I got a clear physical picture of this woman—tall,
dark eyes, hair, and dress—yes, she was Turkish or thereabouts.
She was young, in her twenties, a rounded, smooth face—naive,
yet sensual in a secret, dark way not even she could comprehend.
Her clothes were all black, covering up most of her—conservative,
foreign, like her parents who protected and surrounded her as
they moved away, a Moslem fortress. Yet she belonged to the
reindeer, untamed inside, and I pulled myself together, remembering I was in an American museum.

I thought for a moment maybe all this about her was my
romantic imagination kicking in, but as I moved subtly in her

direction our eyes flicked taut again and the heat firing in my body confirmed the connection. There was a white-hot cord weaving through the display cases. By mutual agreement we kept a distance to keep her wary parents happy. Yet we managed consuming looks through several panes of glass, via mirrors, in orchestrated turnings to a mutual choreographer. In between, we relished the next encounter, tingling energy bouncing off the partitions, as the golden reindeer seemed to shimmer and race along with us. Her parents knew something was in the air and would continually check her. After a volley of the Earth Mother, she would turn to them a childlike, virginal countenance, a very proper shell containing the erotic plains of her blood.

We continued thus, floating through the collection for an hour—Robert and I meeting up once for mutual ooohs and ahhhs about the art. But soon the end was in sight and we made a bold move to end up side by side near the corner case. A large, magnificent, iron reindeer gazed profoundly at us as our energies barely contained the bounds of our bodies. Her hands were slightly shivering on the case and soon our rigid glances surged up together for a final merging release of the stampede—her wild, dark eyes had me and mine swallowed up her passion. I was still standing there resonating, full and wistful, after her angry parents whisked her out the exit, when Robert sauntered up going on and on about the collection. Yes, I mumbled, it is amazing what the Hittite culture produced—I was particularly taken with their sweet reindeer.

SEASON

Sun's pushing back
        winter.
    The new moon kisses
          twilight
              lightly–
Delighting
      how early
         Spring comes here,
      I AM Spring
            this year.

WORK

Watch you working,
       tight jeans
           swooning overby–
    Move hand
       to pluck,
          grasp,
             stroke–no,
  gaze–
        send thought to
        bridge gap body,
             by & by we
    tangling work, untangling
        wire meshed meshing
       of Levi energy
           encased
            among thorns.

Nov. 10, 1980

Dear Sandy,

Greetings friend! Here's to four years of Ronnie and his right-wing capitalist pals. I can't wait for what's in store for gays, blacks, and women. Poor Carter, he was just too much of a nice guy and the hostages did him in in the end. Ronnie would have sent in the cavalry! I wonder what area he'll pick? I bet the Middle East.

I'm in somewhat of a cynical mood as you can tell, probably something to do with reaching the exalted age of 60. I thought 30 was a big deal and traumatic—I ate half an orange that fateful day, but 60! My birthday was a month ago and I still can't relate to being this old. You are one of my few "old" friends, so I have to ask, do you feel strange when you look in the mirror and see all those wrinkles and sagging parts that used to be so firm? I'm having a really hard time (and have been for some while) accepting that that's me. I don't *feel* old, and indeed most of my friends are in the twenties to forties range. No matter what my body is doing I'm still growing mentally and relate more to younger people. Is that deluding myself? I just find that most people my age are very stuck in their habits and, frankly, are boring. In many ways I'm just beginning to figure out what I'm about and what I want to pursue. Life is still a fascinating mystery and I thrive on the inquiry, but we're supposed to have it figured out by now, so "they" say. So I seem to be caught between my physical self and my being self. It's not a comfortable place, and now being single again it's even more scary and perplexing.

It's been six months since I disentangled myself from Jeanine after five years of a relationship that I now see was

91

symbiotic blood-sucking for the most part. It was exciting and intense and intellectual, but it had no heart (or maybe too much heart as in drama and manipulation) or real support for each other. We seemed to be playing out a bizarre fantasy that had actually turned sour by the end of the first year. I am still amazed at myself for having put up with it and playing that perverse game for so long. Do you believe that she was seeing someone a year before we split up, while still claiming she was having a "problem" with me sexually? Give me a break! I definitely see my role in the whole thing—my need for security, my need to take care of someone, my living out a past that was no longer there, but she still thinks it's all my fault and I'm resentful about that. I'm trying to let the whole thing go and start fresh, but it's difficult. I have doubts whether I will at this point in my life find someone to love and with whom I can share my "declining" years.

My music and my teaching have really saved my life during all this time. I have expanded my classes at the Institute and made a leap by committing to a national chamber tour starting next spring with the Philharmonia. It's exciting because I haven't performed extensively for the last five years (too much pressure from Jeanine), so I'm warming up my embouchure and pouring all my emotions into the oboe, which always expresses them so intensely. But the oboe doesn't go to bed with me and there is a large hole when I come home alone and make dinner for one.

I always scoffed at comments that lesbian relationships were unstable and what happens when you get old and have no children to look after you. I never wanted children, but I guess I did expect someone to be around when I got older. I don't know

whether that has anything to do with being a lesbian, though. My aunt is 88, had four husbands, and is still alone as she slowly dies in a nursing home near here. Ironically I, the queer one, am the only member of my family who cares enough to visit her and manage what money she has left. It is really tragic and I never want to find myself in that situation (if I am, please come and put a pillow over my face), but I'll be damned if I'll hang onto a relationship or start one out of a fear of being alone. I've always been independent and I have many close and loving friends, and I'm prepared to go it alone if necessary, but I really do want a lover, a partner with whom I can share the excitement of the rest of my life. As I said, I have my doubts for I find myself attracted mainly to younger women and who would want an old oboist like me (though I do have terrific kissing qualities after 45 years with the double reed!).

So, Sandy, I'm in the emotional dumps facing being an old dyke with dubious grace. I should take some lessons from you who grow wiser and more mellow as the years go by, as I grow more cantankerous and rebellious. I guess our long, long friend-ship has always had that balance in opposites and it has been a mainstay during all my traumas over the years. Lovers seem to come and go, but you dear friend are there forever.

I will be in San Francisco in May with the group and hope to be "over" Jeanine and my 60th birthday slump by then, so we can play in my old territory. Is that old, flea-bitten place, the Rendez-Vous, still there on Potrero? Give my love to Bea and let's hope Reagan doesn't turn out as badly as we all fear!

Your ancient friend,

Sylvia

Time dwells in hurt, sometimes–
                    loitering, dragging
            present thru
                    moments thick
            with pain.

Love seems inexorably ripped,
                past, a bruise thumping
        in the chest,
                        a chest closed,
                enfolded in hurt,
                        time-locked.

And the moment
            trembles,
                in waiting–
                            poised
        to escape the slow march onward
    & fly
                unbound, straight
                    to the joy
                        of now,
                            no time.

Chapter V
THE COMMUNITY

July 21, 1981

Dear Laura,

 I am sitting on a large porch and gazing out on the evening-lit Russian River languidly going by on its way to the ocean. There are redwoods, pine, willow lining the banks and a lawn spreading to the river. The porch is lined with a riot of potted pansies, marigolds, roses. It also has a mixed bouquet of couples—women with women, men with men, and one lone straight couple (?). Everyone interacts with one another, cooking on the grill, singing to the piano inside, and at night we all take turns in the hot tub floating under the clear starry night. This is my favorite of the family resorts up here, our special family that blends effortlessly with the town of Guerneville.

 I wish you had had time to come up here before going back to St. Louis. I sometimes forget that this doesn't exist there, everywhere. It is sad you just can't go to a resort with your lover in most parts of the country and just relax and enjoy it openly. Here is the perfect get-away from the city, especially if you're gay. I come up alone mostly, to contemplate, read, hike in the redwoods, and generally ground out all the city nerves I've accumulated. If one feels like it, there are a few wild dancing establishments, which are especially hot over the summer weekends, and resorts for men with special tastes. But mostly we escapees just want to get some sun, canoe and hike, and party quietly with our lovers and friends.

 The town looks like Anytown, Anywhere, America—Main St., Pat's Diner, Lark Drugs, the 5 &10, and sandwiched in there is the Rainbow Cattle Co., a gay men's bar. The straight townspeople are warm and down-to-earth and don't seem to mind the gays and the gays are respectful of them. And being a little over an hour from San Francisco, this is an easy place to vacate to. A wonderful state park is nearby, full of the most magnificent redwoods. One feels like a penitent there, humbled—the forest is my personal church when I'm up here. Up the hill the mountains range as far as the eye can see, with endless miles to hike. Over the years I've come to know a lot of the local gays, resort owners, waitresses. It's nice to catch up and visit with them, even as I spend most of my time alone. The sun is getting close to setting now, so I think I'll go to the ocean to see it splash, get a great meal at a friend's restaurant, then maybe shake a leg at the Woods and see if any other single ladies are floating around!

I am telling you all this to make you pea-green with envy and so you'll move from your city suburb, where you have to play straight (from your last letter you don't sound very happy there), to the gay nirvana in this area of California, which is so very beautiful. Just ask yourself this question: Wouldn't you love to walk down the street of a small town at night, arm around your lady, and not be afraid of a carload of goons coming along and yelling, "Dykes" or "Why don't you try us?" or worse? Think about it, friend.

Love you,
Diane

Oct. 9, 1984

Dear Mom and Dad,

I am alone in a cabin up at the Stanislaus River for a few days. I needed to get away from everyone. The sympathy was too much, even though my friends meant well. It's over. Martin is gone, and while part of me is relieved that his pain is over, the greater part is just now realizing that I will never see him again. Mom and Dad, he was my best friend, he was like a brother. No, we were closer than siblings, he knew me thoroughly, better perhaps than you, for he was my peer. And he's gone and I feel a huge, ragged hole in me and I am lost in it. I am numb and yet hurt all over. I don't understand, and there is anger just under the wall of grief. I am afraid of life without my nearest compatriot. Why did he have to die and so horribly? For the first time in six months there is no action, I am alone with it and I walk aimlessly around this beautiful place in search of something with meaning, bleeding silently. I need to write my anguish to you, you are the only ones left I am truly close to.

I suppose if Martin had a heart attack like Uncle Charles or went in a car accident like Liz, his death would be easier to accept. But no, he died of AIDS, that deadly disease that has struck gay men, snatching them quickly.

In March, as you know, I went to New York immediately when Joe told me Martin had cancer. A few days later I was there in the room with his mother when the diagnosis was said. Martin and I walked down Christopher St. back to his place arm-in-arm, so close with our love which was now threatened. For the first time in New York I saw the moon in the sky. It was a half moon. Not saying anything we drank in the sights and sounds of the street, walking slowly. We were strangely calm with the knowledge, and when we got to his place he said he didn't want to prolong his life if it came down to lingering and pain. He said he wanted pills. He never got them, and over the months we all tried every hope and method that existed. In the end he fought endless depression and pain for just a few more weeks, days, and then it claimed him.

AIDS, why did it come and why can't they cure it? It is a gruesome disease, eating away the body's defenses. The religious fanatics say it is God's wrath and punishment for homosexuals' evil ways. I get so enraged with that logic. What did the Legionnaires do wrong for their disease? Goddamn self-righteous bigots. Men are dying like flies from this unknown virus, which happened to start in the gay community, and all they can think about is judging them and taking delicious glee in their misfortune. I can't think of anything more un-Christian than that. Straight America better wake up now because it hardly is a disease for gay males only. It is deadly for all of us and it's spreading from the gay community fast.

The male community here is terrified. I would say that the majority of gay men are in a tense state of waiting (the incubation period is a long time). Meanwhile, they tend to their friends and lovers who do know. There is a pall over what was once one of the liveliest areas in town, the Castro. I have many male gay friends, and especially over the last six months I've been eyeing them for ill-health, asking them outright if they are being safe. I am scared they will all go.

But Martin, he was special, and God I miss him and God I hurt, Mom and Dad. He was so talented and bright and I loved him so much. To watch him waste away and look at me with those sunken eyes for help, for an answer. It haunts me, my helplessness in the face of his dying. I gave him all the love I could, as did Joe and his mother and his friends. But it wasn't enough. I am lost without him, especially with Uncle Charles and Liz, my other closest buddy, having gone so recently. You are the only ones from my past. I feel I am losing myself, my perspective, my mirrors of who I am out of who I was. Martin knew all of me— we traveled around the world together singing Janis Joplin songs through the Persian desert, we walked the rocks at Gloucester in the fall, we came out together, and we laughed and cried together from such knowing love. What am I going to do without him?

I need you, Mom and Dad. I need to come home soon and feel your love fill some of the hole in me. I really appreciated your support during the whole ordeal and I know Martin's mother was glad for your letters and calls. I don't know if I would have been as strong without you. Thank you. So after I finish my project at work next month I would like to stay with you from Thanksgiving until New Year's. I know that's an imposition but I need the shelter and healing of being home with you for a while. I know time heals all wounds, and this one will take a long, long time. I hope to God the government moves fast to fund the AIDS research. It's not just the gays who are fighting for their lives. We're all in this together and we must stop this loss of our loved ones. Thanks for listening. Be in contact soon.

I love you, Jennifer

P.S. Please have Rev. Scott say a prayer for Martin at St. Christopher's. Thanks.

THE COMMUNITY

BAR SCENE

Journal
June 12, 1975

    She came into the bar. The pause following the close of the door brought scrutiny, so she kept on moving to the end of the counter, saying hello to the bartender, and without looking, sensed the cliques tonight. She in turn was being absorbed by the ladies, not yet ready for consumption, but still on the menu. She was not quite sure whether she was an appetizer, a main course, or a dessert to them. She just knew she was there and she wanted to relax and be herself and be with people, women people. She also knew it was unlikely when she felt the knot of the last two days tighten at the back of her neck as she ordered a Jack Daniels over. The bartender was entangled in that knot—blond, flirtatious, a recent lover who loved being behind that counter.

    The others felt distant to her, as most of the audible conversation went from softball to who was sleeping with whom and back again. She could give a shit, and ached for some communication where there was some real joy and concern, one woman sharing with another. However, the menu seemed set— hamburger, fries, and a draft.

    The top-twenty disco music throbbed, the cue ball teetered on the corner pocket and she sat alone, long jeaned legs crossed, closed. "Why the hell should I be the one to put it out there," she thought. "It only gets trampled on anyway." She played being aloof and bored, when in fact she felt like shouting, "You idiots, if all you're interested in is sexual gossip and pool, then you're no better than the straight men you condemn! Stop it!" Her cry was stifled underneath the fear of just that game. She found some familiar women to be with, chatting and gossiping.

She, at least, was distracted from her dismal thoughts for a while. She chastised herself for her judgments and yet they remained. After three quick drinks she beat a retreat out and into herself. Not before she uneasily asked the bartender out for dinner.

It was dark out and the Bay Bridge as usual offered comfort in speed with much thinking.

June 14, 1985

Dear Sue,

It's exciting that you're going to San Francisco this summer! Of course I'll fill you in on "the scene" as we were just there in April and had a ball. First of all, the weather is unpredictable, sunny one minute and cloudy or rainy the next, so always bring a jacket when you go out. It always seemed cool to us, but then we are used to the steamy, hot South. In the summer it should be warmer, but I heard the fog can roll in and it gets cold again. But the city is even more gorgeous than the postcards show and you must do all the touristy things like the cable cars, Alcatraz, Fisherman's Wharf, and so on.

As to the "other" tourist side of San Francisco, there is lots to do! First of all you must go to the Castro and to Polk St. and just watch the boys cruising around (and some girls) in their tank tops or outrageous leather outfits or whatever. It is remarkable for a whole area of town to be primarily gay and to have been able to walk down the street with my arm around Doris—it felt weird but good (I actually kissed her on the street one night!). In most areas of town I saw gay couples and it was so refreshing, coming from the repressed (mostly) southern attitude.

As to the bar scene, a bar is a bar is a bar, and Doris and I don't hang out in them normally. But we did taste the different types because we wanted to meet women in the gay capital of the world and to see what we were missing.

The best and classiest bar is called Clementina's, on Folsom St. Mostly couples go there and we saw all types, from leather punks to businesswomen to hotly dressed ladies. The front part is a big bar and small tables with a small stage where they have live entertainment during the week—nice cabaret stuff. Brick walls and a high ceiling give it a clean, respectable look and make all the bars in New Orleans seem even more dingy than they are. The back has a large dance floor and smaller bar with a D.J. booth and great sound system. On the Saturday we were there the place was hopping with hordes of the *best-looking* women I've ever seen in one place. Doris and I looked at each other at one point and laughed because we could tell we both had a slight longing to be single again. No chance! It was a treat, though, to look at all that gorgeous womanhood and we felt comfortable there. By all means go there first!

Then there is Amelia's, about ten minutes away from Clementina's, on Valencia. The atmosphere is completely different. It is a primo pick-up place and packed at all hours any day of the week with mostly Latin and black women (a younger group) who are there to boogie. It is much more down-to-earth and sensual, but still much more up than what is here. I was amazed at some of the types of women there. One woman I swore was a man from behind—a well-muscled back and shoulders and a marine haircut, along with leopard tights and a tank top—until "he" turned around and I was confronted with an enormous pair of tits! No way that was from hormone shots! She was the butchest-looking woman (from the back) I've ever seen, but with those wild tights and muscles she had a preppy pair of glasses that looked absurd under the marine cut. And one woman had a shaved head (looked like a martian) and one was dressed in leather from head to toe—you've just got to go and watch the show. Don't worry, there are plenty of "normal" women and it's fun to jostle around and dance.

Then there's Peg's Place on Geary, your basic neighborhood bar of locals. Much more our style and pleasant enough with a large pool table area, a jukebox, and a small dance floor in the back. It's a place to stop off and have a drink after work, alone or with a friend. There are some other bars but frankly we just didn't have the energy to check them all out. Use your *Gaia's Guide* for a complete listing or call the Gay Hotline.

That's just the bar scene. The wonderful thing about San Francisco is they have a full women's culture there. It's not limited to bars, as in most cities. They have large lesbian business organizations and networks, legal assistance groups, medical clinics, counseling, and so on. They even have women's body-building contests—I'm sorry we missed seeing one!

You'll have no problem entertaining yourself (I recommend taking vitamins, in fact) and I hope my suggestions help in directing your trip. Have fun and give the Golden Gate Bridge and the ladies at Amelia's a hug for me. I think we all leave a bit of our hearts in San Francisco! Write me when you get back!

Love,

March 10, 1985

Dear Clarence,

How's my favorite preacher doing? I know I haven't been to church for three weeks (lots of sins are piling up), but my life has been so busy the last month. I'll try to make it next Sunday and for sure on Easter. Since it's hard to talk to you on Sundays and virtually impossible to get you on the phone, I am writing to you about a dilemma I find myself in, and I would appreciate some advice from you.

I have started a correspondence with a cousin of mine in Illinois who is concerned about her daughter being a lesbian. I guess I have become the family gay consultant since, as everyone knows through the grapevine, I am "out." We've had an honest and moving correspondence and she is trying to understand the choice of homosexuality for her daughter Sally and all of us in general. In her last letter she brought up the bottomline reasons for her inability to accept homosexuality (even as she "loves Sally and me"), and they come from her religious beliefs. Now that I've started going to church again, I feel like I'm as "good" a Christian as anyone, but I have developed no religious arguments to respond to her religious beliefs, and I feel I need some ammo from a good source, i.e., you, a gay Episcopal priest. By the way, I don't know if I've ever thanked you for opening up the Episcopal Church for me again. I used to think everyone religious felt as my cousin feels, but you have shown me there is indeed room for gays in the Church. I have gotten a lot of nourishment spiritually from rejoining it. Thank you. Anyway, I'm not trying to convert her, but I want her to consider other valid ways of seeing homosexuality in a religious context. She really means well and I think she wants to understand better, but I feel unqualified and frankly scared to come up against Jesus according to her experience of Him. Help! I will quote parts of her letter so you can see where she's coming from:

"First, you must know that I am a true believer in Christ, our Father, and the Holy Spirit. I read the Bible every day. I do not think of myself as a born-again Christian because I have always loved my Lord and have become stronger in my faith as time goes by. The Bible talks about unnatural relationships in both the Old and the New Testaments. Specifically, the very clear and well-known Sodom and Gomorrah story, the passage from Leviticus, Chapter 20, Verse 13, 'If a man also lie with mankind, as he lieth with a woman, both of them have committed an abomination: they shall surely be put to death: their blood shall be upon them,' and St. Paul's reference to homosexuality as against God's wishes. It is clear from the Bible that homosexuality is a sin and cannot be condoned as being natural. It is not. Sally and I have had long talks about this. I have told her that I cannot accept her choice of sexual relationships. And I have told her that I love her and I respect her mind, but I would be telling her a lie if I said I accepted her way of life. As amazing as it sounds we are 'best' friends and we respect each other. We also love each other dearly. We enjoy being with each other a great deal.

"The love between a man and woman is God-given. First, I think of the mental give and take. Two women can never have this kind of communication because they are two women. Second, the sexual act of intercourse was made to be one that fits. A man-to-man or a woman-to-woman intercourse doesn't fit. Although I can imagine what it must be like not to have a sexual attraction for the opposite sex but only to your own, I thank God that I don't have that. This is cruel to you and to Sally, but I must be honest and tell you how I feel. I tell you this openly because this act was made not only to satisfy our lust but also to have babies. To have babies through artificial insemination and to bring them up in an all-female world bothers me greatly. Naturally there is no way we will see the end to this family setup or how it will affect the child or anything. And I know that there are plenty of people living in homes set up this way. But God help us! Anyway, to have and raise children with your husband is something that can never be replaced by a man-man relationship or a woman-woman relationship. I must admit that I have often hoped that Sally might have the kind of relationships Vita Sackville-West experienced. Her marriage to Sir Harold Nicolson, her two boys, and then her other relationships with Violet Trefusis and later Virginia Woolf. It still is not or was not the best answer, I suppose. . . .

"Now Joan, please do not think of me as being a narrow-minded old woman. I read and I listen and I always hope I'll have an open mind and be able to learn. But because of my faith I have tremendous difficulty with the gay movement. Because of my faith I am always hopeful and pray everyday that my darling Sally can be turned in some way. I pray the same for you."

See what I mean? I could use prayers for lots of things, but I don't need them for being a lesbian. God knows that. She really is a wonderful person and I would appreciate getting together with you for some gay religious doctrine before I see her. I'm sure you are an expert on the subject! Hope things are going better with Jeff. The last time I saw you two it looked iffy. I'm in the same boat as you with Carol. Let's have a two-part get-together, religion and relationship at Cafe Flore. Thanks cutie.

Take care, Joan

111

March 18,1985

Dear Joan,

Yes, I have missed you and Carol in church lately and I admit to being difficult to reach at home, mostly because of Jeff or church groups every night. Your letter was very moving in that you want to respond to your cousin in a loving way that keeps the channel of communication open with her. I have, obviously, dealt with the issue of homosexuality in respect to Christianity and I will give you some abbreviated comments on the issue.

First, I would recommend that your cousin read *Time for Consent: A Christian's Approach to Homosexuality*. It is written by a well-known Anglican clergyman at King's College, Norman Pittenger. His basic message and one that I and the Episcopal Church now espouse is: Jesus' message to us was love–pure, simple, and unconditional. And as such, the only sin is in not loving, period. When we cut off our love for one another by judging or condemning others, their lifestyles, sexuality, religious beliefs, and so on, we are sinning, not they. Relationships entered into with love, respect, and intention therefore, are not sinful no matter who the people are.

Jesus nowhere mentions homosexuality. He was here to teach us about loving God and one another. Your cousin refers to the Bible in respect to her condemnation of homosexuality. The Sodom and Gomorrah story is now interpreted not as a condemnation of homosexuality but of a general breaking of the strict Jewish social codes that existed at the time. The town as a whole had long been unruly and disrespectful, and God brought his wrath down on their last act of disregard for Lot's hospitality, not because they were homosexuals. And the reference from

Leviticus. This comes in the middle of a long list of Jewish rules, which include condemning the violation of strict dietary laws, contacting women in their menstrual cycle, cursing one's parents, nakedness, and many other minutiae that are mostly inappropriate for modern day interpretation. If we were as strict in our interpretation of the other passages as in that of homosexuality, then we'd be living as we did before Christ, and dashing in the heads of Babylonian babies and other such things.[1] Such out-of-context moralizing in God's name is in my opinion self-righteous harassment born of personal prejudices. And St. Paul's comments are more a reflection of his Jewish background in which homosexuality is, as seen in the licentious context of the Roman Empire of his time, tied to the human tendency of idolatry.[2] All of these references are really condemning pure lust and a human self-centeredness that takes away from our loving God. They are no longer interpreted (by most) as referring to loving relationships between two people of the same sex.

I find it sad that there are many gay people who want to be part of the Church again, but are fearful of the Falwell types who go on about how sinful and unnatural homosexuality is. I'm glad you have seen that is not the case in the Episcopal Church and have gotten value out of celebrating Christ in the Church again. I am trying to reach more gay people for we especially need our faith in these often oppressive times, and the Church has come a long way in providing a more loving (and nonsexist) environment for our worship of God. I sometimes get disheartened when in the name of Christ (again, whose message was only love), such hatred is sown, and by people who call themselves devout Christians. Point that out to your cousin. It should give her pause.

I hope these thoughts help in your correspondence with

her. You are in a good place of not condemning in return, but showing her a loving way to see it differently. I am doing well, but working too many hours, which drives Jeff crazy. I don't know if he has the patience for being a priest's partner in the long run. I hope so for I dearly love him. We'll see. Hope all is well with you and Carol. Let's have lunch soon!

Much love,

CLARENCE

---

[1] Norman Pittenger, *Time for Consent: A Christian's Approach to Homosexuality* (London: SCM Press, 1976), 84.

[2] Ibid., 82.

Aug. 2, 1983

Dear Lesbian Legal Union,

I am a 36-year-old lesbian and I have just been "laid off" from my 12-year job with Central Railroad. I am sure it is because I'm gay. They officially said they were cutting back on personnel for budgetary reasons and did lay off about 15 people, but none had the seniority I had, and because of the harassment I've gotten over the last year, I'm sure it was for other reasons. Let me explain.

For most of the 12 years I worked for CR, I had really no hassles except for the usual macho stuff I got being one of two women in an all-male crew. I was the first woman on the work crew and was proud of that. At first I had to put up with an enormous amount of grief. They pushed my work load to the max, riding me the whole time, but I hung in there, doing at least 50 percent more real work than they did and giving as good as I got. After six months Stan, the foreman, softened up and kind of took me under his wing (he and I over the years became close buddies and I'm sure he knew I was gay, but it didn't seem to bother him). Eventually they all respected me and I was one of the gang. In my third year I was even invited by the guys to join the company baseball team and I became their star shortstop. It caused a ruckus in the league at the time, but the gang was on my side and I played and joined in all the postgame beer parties. When it came to other events with the wives, though, I would usually beg off and be with my mysterious, possessive boyfriend Al. I was in the closet for good reason—most of them are bigoted about gays. Then a year ago I got promoted to an office job and I was excited about the higher pay and doing something more

117

white collar. Now, again, I was in the closet and pretended I lived with my boyfriend Al (Alice).

The office group was much different and there were more serious passes made at me from the first, and when I didn't put out, there were implied threats of repercussions. In particular my boss, Gus Freeman, really gave me a hard time and threatened to put me back on a crew in the roughest area of town if I didn't sleep with him. He is a real pig. I was scared and pissed at the same time because I wanted to keep the job and couldn't really talk to anyone about it. I did bring it up with one of the other women, but she just said to ignore it (she's married).

Finally, one day Gus actually cornered me in his office and after trying to get away for some time I lost it and told him I wasn't interested in any goddamn man and to get away from me. He stopped and said, "You're a dyke?" I ran out while I had the chance. From then on the office was hell. I was making friends and all of a sudden they got distant and started whispering behind my back. I was isolated and it was difficult to do my work. I was frightened. Gus at first ignored me, but then one day he cornered me again saying, "What you need is a man, you queer!" At that point I kneed him and ran out again. Two weeks later I was "laid off."

From what I've read in the paper, this is sexual discrimination of two sorts and I want to know if I can sue that creep or CR. I don't know whether I want my job back with all that went down, but I've been very depressed because of the emotional violence that was done to me. I did love working there for most of the time. The job had good benefits, and I was a loyal and hardworking employee. I've kept in touch with Stan and a couple of the gang who were cool about it, and told them what's coming down.

They were sympathetic, as I cried in my beer, but can't do much. And I'm scared about finding a good-paying job before my unemployment runs out. Alice and I might have to move because my salary paid most of the rent. She supports her family a lot. Our relationship is really uptight since I lost the job and I'm confused, pissed, and scared by the whole thing in general. It seems so unfair to lose it all because I'm gay and wouldn't sleep with the boss. I hope you can help me.

Please write or call me and tell me if I have a case and if so, could you represent me, as I am low on money.

Thanks,

LAURA P.

Aug. 15, 1983

Dear Laura,

   Thank you for your letter dated August 2, 1983. We are sympathetic to your circumstances, and indeed receive many requests for help in the area of sexual orientation discrimination at place of work. Unfortunately, because of the number of such requests, and the limits of our staff time and funding, we are unable to take on your potential cause of action at this time.
   We do, however, have recommendations about whom you could go to for legal assistance. First of all, if you belong to a union, contact them. It is their job to protect you from unfair practices, but know that some unions will take on this sort of case and some will refuse. If the union is uncooperative, then we can put you in contact with many legal assistance groups. We can also recommend some attorneys familiar with that area of law who might take on your case on a contingency fee basis.
   From what you described in your letter it seems as if you do have two sorts of discrimination actionable by you against your employer, as a woman and as a lesbian. Your attorney should look into the many possibilities of claims under federal and state laws that deal with discrimination and/or wrongful discharge. We are available to consult with your attorney about these courses of action and which might be most fruitful for you.
   While we hope that you will eventually prevail if you pursue legal action, we caution you that the process is long, very costly in time, money, and emotional stress, and the outcome is uncertain. You are fortunate to live in California for the laws are much stronger here. However, the judge and jury are still likely to be straight and less than sympathetic. Also, the burden of proof

will be on you to show that your boss and/or the company actively discriminated against you (i.e., witnesses to your encounters with your boss, office gossip, employee contracts, personnel records, and so on).

We know you have been through a difficult time and there should be clear-cut, fast action you could take. Unfortunately legal action involving sexual discrimination of any sort is very difficult to pin down and is without much precedent. We recommend that you look long and hard at what you want to achieve, your stamina, and your financial resources before you take on a long legal battle. If you choose to do so we will give you the names of some support networks of people who could help you through the process. Again, we will be glad to refer you to competent lawyers or legal assistance programs and lend them our expertise in the matter. Do contact your union first though, and let us know if we can be of further assistance.

Sincerely,

Joanna Hardy
Staff Attorney

JH/cd

May 12, 1985

Dear Kathy,

Thanks for your amicus brief on the Madison case, which will really help in our overall brief combining the Lesbian Legal Union and the Gay Rights Project for the big hearing in July with the INS in federal court. Of course we feel strongly it is discriminatory and unconstitutional, barring "known" homosexuals from entering the U.S., but the law is already in place and it will take a sledgehammer to change it. I sometimes envy your having only a small percentage of pro bono work for lesbian rights. I'm in the thick everyday, if not in court then worrying about raising money to keep the Union alive.

Yes, we have made great progress over our five years in child custody cases, in military cases, and in job discrimination, not to mention our general educative services and preventive law. And sometimes it gets very discouraging. Did you hear about the Massachusetts case involving two gay foster parents? They lost in court and out of that was passed a law barring lesbians and gays from being foster parents. As if that wasn't bad enough, they are now trying to get a law through to bar adoption by gays—and Massachusetts is a liberal state. What a horrible precedent! Of course, the law is being challenged as unconstitutional and we have great hope of overturning it, but that will take time.

And the Iowa case is really sad. I don't know if you know about it, so I'll brief you in case you have some connections there. Jane and Dorothy, a couple, were living together for seven years. Dorothy had a bad accident and was severely brain-damaged. The prognosis was slow recovery over a period of years and Jane applied for guardianship of her. Dorothy's parents, asserting Jane "would take advantage of her state," fought the application and got guardianship. They put her in a home and denied Jane visitation rights. Can you imagine! Jane has been very courageous in fighting for and winning some visitation rights in court over the last year and a half. She is still pressing for guardianship, saying that the home doesn't take care of her well (she is often unbathed and her bedding is a mess when Jane visits) and that her progress has been slowed because she is not near her partner. The parents assert that Jane upsets Dorothy and impedes her recovery. Jane is bravely slugging away, but it's hard to fight parents. So if you know of anyone out there to throw some weight, please call me. It may be a matter of life or death.

Thanks again for your input to our brief. Sorry I've cried on your shoulder a bit, but lawyering for a cause is often tough going (like always). The gains and overall progress to women, however, make it the only game in town for me.

Give my love to Marsha and hope to see you soon!

All my best,

Shelly

Feb. 9, 1984

Dear Clarissa,

I feel sick to my stomach—so mad and so powerless at the same time that I have to vomit the outrage somehow. Remember I called you two weeks ago about the tragedy of my friend Marian's death? I am still in shock about it. At least we know now the drunk will get a stiff sentence and be off the road for a long time, but it's too late for Marian. The tragedy has expanded though for her lover Terry in a most cruel way. Marian's parents kicked her out of the house, the house they lived in for twelve years, *two* days after Marian's death! Not only that, her parents are trying to claim their cafe, both cars, and virtually everything they had in common. Terry is staying at Susan's for now and is so numb she can't fight back at the moment. I've called my lawyer and have been working with her to establish communal rights for Terry, but without a will and being a gay couple (every gay couple should have a will), there's a lot that would have to be proven by oral agreements, their financial interactions, witnesses, etc. Most judges are still straight, male, and conservative, and would prefer to go with the parents as next of kin. But those two knew half of San Francisco and half of San Francisco had been to their house over the years, so with a lot of oral confirmations and doing our homework we think we can put together a decent case.

The problem is, the house was given to Marian by her grandparents, and she did start off with more money, but they shared everything equally, gave each other gifts, and the business, though mostly funded initially by Marian, was really jointly theirs from the start. However, there is "nothing in writing." And her greedy, middle class parents, who barely acknowledged

Marian because she was a lesbian and certainly not Terry, now are claiming it all. They assert Terry was living totally off Marian and in fact was a bad influence on their darling daughter who tragically died at 42. It makes me want to throw up. I just can't believe that Marian's parents can be so unfeeling and ignore their relationship, which was the most stable, fun, and happy I've ever known, of any combination. Those two were an institution, and to throw Terry in the garbage heap with nothing after losing her mate, to me, is criminal. So in the midst of our grief, all our friends are going to fight like hell to get her at least the half of the property she deserves.

Did you know that next month they were planning to celebrate their thirteenth anniversary by cruising around the Caribbean for two weeks on a female-crewed yacht? All Terry has to look forward to now is grief, a messy legal battle, and finding a job. I'm sick for her and I'm so saddened by the inhumanity of Marian's parents. Unfortunately there's a lot of that going on, particularly with parents of gay men, who of course are dying off fast from AIDS. I wish our community would wise up and get as much legal protection as they can before tragedy strikes.

Thank God not all parents are monsters, though. Case in point, my dear, dear friend Mark, who died two years ago in Phoenix. He had been with his lover Ricardo for four years and they had a condominium and a business together as well as other property. Mark was afraid, during the six months he was sick, that his parents, who held the note on the condo, would shaft Ricardo when he died. They assured him they wouldn't, stuck by him through thick and thin with Ricardo, and honored his wishes after he died, keeping up a close relationship with Ricardo. It was a tragedy as well to lose him so young, but the love and support that was there all around (brothers and sisters included) made it a more bearable and dignified death process.

Death of a mate is the hardest to bear, particularly in our community, with straight families often trying to usurp our partnership rights after the death of our loved ones. There is a lot of work to be done legally and moralistically. I intend to do my share—right now, for poor Terry. Is the situation in Florida any better, and do you and Sharon have a will?

Onward! I'll call you soon.

Love,

Joyce

Nov. 2, 1981

Dear Helen,

As always it was sure great to see you, dear friend. It doesn't seem to matter how many years intervene or what we've been doing, we pick up as though we were still freshmen in Lathrop Dorm, studying all night, fighting for the pay phone, and talking about the secrets of life (and boys, always). I don't have many friends in my life like you who have seen me through many seasons, so I bathed and drank deep of you during my visit.

Some observations and questions you had in the women's bars that we went to in Boston stimulated some thoughts I have had about the lesbian community. I'd like to expand on them and see where I get.

You as a straight woman observed that many lesbians seem (at least in public) to have a cautious or tough attitude that is theirs as a minority group but not necessarily theirs as individuals. And you thought that many purposely dress down and hide their beauty because of this attitude and that that was detrimental to our image. I had mixed feelings about what you said. Even though I understand that this attitude exists because of the unfair treatment of homosexuals in our society, I don't feel it is really productive for the community at large, either.

As you are well aware, we women are struggling to gain equality in the job market and the male-dominated world in general. We have made some progress, but if one is a lesbian, everything is threatened by the gratuitous discrimination that most of straight society lays on us. It seems silly that we are judged across the board by whom we sleep with, but there it is. And it is very real, with lesbians fearing the loss of their jobs, their children, their respect among friends and family. So it is no wonder that some lesbians carry a defensive/offensive attitude. It's often necessary for us to do so in this world.

As to the way lesbians dress, I think in general we reject the accepted ideas and the advertising hoopla of what is "feminine." We don't need to impress each other with fashion and perhaps we don't want men to hassle us. As a group on the fringe of society we have our own standards and values that give us strength and identity. Yet I feel there are some innate limitations that impede our progress as individuals and a community.

I sometimes notice in myself an awareness, a caution that others may react strongly to my lesbianism. It is understandably a stance that I think we as homosexuals all have to some degree. And, in the extreme, it becomes the chip-on-the-shoulder attitude of "I AM A LESBIAN AND YOU BETTER LIKE IT" or a fearful silence to live in. I don't believe it's healthy to *be* our sexual identity, however, for that seems to encourage the separation of gay and straight, the offense/defense. I think any person or group of people who, even unconsciously, plays the "my identity vs. your identity" game really enforces prejudice and alienation.

God knows homosexuality has come a very long way from the dark closet days of even twenty years ago. A strong gay community and political movement are waking people up to the fact that we exist, we are everywhere, and we demand our rights as proud members of society. And, I think there is still a tendency for some lesbians to cling to the community, to maintain the separate attitude, to be really uncomfortable in the larger community. If we could all put aside some of our defensiveness, our fears, and be more open and honest with our families, friends, and co-workers, what a difference it would make.

I think that this is happening slowly but surely. It is tough to let go of the anger and a certain reverse-discrimination, to be firmly ourselves in the face of adverse opinion. From what I can see the easiest way to be equal is just that: *be* equal with no excuses, and people will start treating you that way. So while the political activism and the social camaraderie in the community are crucial to us as a minority, I feel we also need to go to beyond our enclave and individually heal the separation that exists in our personal lives.

So, Helen, I took your remarks and clarified what I personally see and feel about the lesbian community. I hope my expounding has broadened your view of it as well. Who would have ever thought back in college we'd be having this sort of conversation? I find it amazing we're 42 as well! Again, it was so special to see you—your turn for a visit next!

Much
Love
Virginia

Dear Mom and Dad,   Sept. 26, 1985

Greetings into this rich fall season! I hope you are both well and enjoying the beginning of the bouquet of color that must be occurring now. I really miss the farm this time of year with its kaleidoscope of intense leaves, the harvested fields, and the start of the crisp air at night. Here we get a few bushes and trees that turn and you can feel the subtle change of season, but it's not the same visually.

Inside, however, I do feel a dramatic shift as of the autumnal equinox, for Diana and I have decided to have a public ceremony in celebration of our union and life commitment to each other, in other words, a wedding! I know you will probably wonder, what does this ceremony mean for us? We have only known each other nine months and lived together three. But when you know you have met your life partner, there is no real questioning (and didn't you know each other just six months before marrying during the war?). We want the "world" (our friends and families) to witness our love and vows to each other. We are ecstatic!

I must admit I did have a few periods of lone-ranger resistance with Diana out of my old framework of not quite believing I, a lesbian, could have the equivalent of marriage. However, we have both broken through to the truth of our enormous strength in loving each other as individuals united for a lifetime. I know you probably have a little difficulty accepting this announcement in quite the same way you would an engagement if I were with a man, but know it is precisely with the same joy and commitment that we are coming together. I know that you liked Diana immensely when you visited this summer and saw how good we are for each other (Dad, I thought you were going to take her back to Ohio with you!), so it is my hope that you will welcome her into the family and join us for our celebration along with her family from Texas and our friends.

The ceremony/ritual will be on the vernal equinox, March 21 of next year, close to Easter. We chose that date intentionally to combine the two spiritual "religions" we bring to the relationship. I have, as you know, refound my spiritual niche in the Church. The teachings of Christ (without the narrow interpretations some people have put on Him), the traditions that I grew up with in the family, and the unity of the congregation each Sunday in a common spirit are very important to me. For Diana her spiritual needs are met in worshipping The Goddess, the Earth Mother, in rituals with other women that more recognize the female aspect of the One Spirit. You are probably unfamiliar with the fact that there is a resurgence of what the Christian church has called paganism or witchcraft, this worship of The Goddess. I have participated in many of the rituals and spiritual gatherings with Diana and they are wonderful, warm celebrations of our relationship to the Earth, to the Universe, and to our fellow (Wo)Man. Women mostly participate in this more matriarchal spirituality, and though many would deem it sacrilegious, I experience it as a powerful alternative to what many of us see as a patriarchal world that closes off our instinctual side. Diana has come to church with me and sees the value of the service, which has become less sexist and dogmatic. We are blending our patriarchal and matriarchal spiritualities into our relationship just as we have balanced the masculine and feminine aspects of ourselves and in how we interact with each other, i.e., no strict roles that we feel impede traditional relationships.

So we have asked my minister, who is gay (and who with others is putting together a liturgy for homosexuals similar to a traditional marriage that they hope will be accepted by the Church hierarchy), and Diana's spiritual teacher to perform a combined ceremony/ritual on the day and in the season of renewal and rebirth. They are both delighted. We have met once with them and looked at many interesting ways to blend the traditions. We see it as being out-of-doors in a green place with lots of spring flowers (and a sheltered place nearby if it rains). An altar will be set up with flowers, candles, incense, a cross, a chalice, and other symbols of both religions. The music Diana and I will tape. It will be a combination of traditional organ pieces and some of the beautiful spiritual music that has come out recently. There will be invocations to The Goddess and the spirits of the four directions as well as to God and the Holy Spirit. Diana and I are working on our vows with them, which we want to be a beautiful and powerful synthesis that embodies our love and vision as we say them to each other. And at the end, after the blessings, we will have our family tradition of the bagpiper leading us out, followed by Diana's family tradition of a wonderful barbeque!

I know that you have worried about me, especially when I told you I was a lesbian, ever finding a mate, someone to share my life with, to grow old with. Diana is that life partner for me, and I look forward to sharing that joy and certainty with you in person when we come for Thanksgiving. I have a lot to be thankful for this year. I can't wait to show Diana the farm, the village and have her meet all the people special to me there. Her parents are coming here next month and they sound like delightful people. I think both sets of "in-laws" will get along just fine.

Now, Mom, I can tell you're already wondering what to wear for such an unusual and momentous occasion, and what your role is in it, and what to tell your friends. When we get there we'll have more of an idea what the ceremony and, of course, the bash to follow will be like, so relax. In the meantime, enjoy the fall and rejoice with us!

Write soon and tell me if that oak tree by the pond is as glorious as ever in its changing prime. Diana sends her love and an extra hug for you, Dad! And, in my happiness, I send

all my love to you,
Jennifer

ACKNOWLEDGMENTS

There are many people I would like to thank for helping me in writing this book of letters. It was my dear friend Linda Goldstone who lead me to Elizabeth Neeld, my masterful writing coach. Elizabeth and Linda opened up my bashful creativity, supported my lines of vision, and were there when I just couldn't write one more word. Thank you.

To all my friends, my family, to all those, known and unknown, whose lives and experience have been woven into the fabric of this book, thank you for your inspiration and courage. To all those who have helped in the production of the book, especially my manuscript readers and my copyeditor, David Sweet, many thanks. And for those of you, having read this book, who see the harsh lines of separation between "gay" and "straight" begin to disappear, I am deeply moved.

Christine Heron Stockton